**A Communication
Audit Handbook**
Helping
Organizations
Communicate

A Communication Audit Handbook
Helping Organizations Communicate

Seymour Hamilton

Consultant Editor: William Beaver

Pitman

PITMAN PUBLISHING
128 Long Acre, London WC2E 9AN

© Longman Group UK Ltd 1987

First published in Great Britain 1987

British Library Cataloguing in Publication Data
Hamilton, S. C.
A communication audit handbook: helping organizations communicate.
1. Communication in management
2. Communication in organizations
I. Title
658.4′5   HD30.3

ISBN 0 273 02829 4

Printed and bound in Great Britain at the Bath Press, Avon
Typeset by Blackmore Press, Longmead, Shaftesbury, Dorset

Contents

Preface

This handbook is a guide on how to assess and improve communication within an organization. It offers information, techniques and a case study to help analyze an organization's communication and information systems. Most importantly, it explains how a well conducted audit will show an organization how it can communicate better.

This is a handbook for people who want to improve internal communication in specific, individual businesses. It will be particularly helpful to you if you are:

- a communication consultant interested in extending your skills;
- a member of in-house communication personnel, planning the use of a contracted communication auditor;
- an executive unaware of what to expect from a communication audit; or
- a student of communication management, wishing to learn how to apply theory to real-life experience.

With this guide you can work out where you are, where to go for important things to do, see and think about, and how to remain poised and competent in what may be an unfamiliar environment. It will give you the chance to decide in advance what you want to do with your time, money and energy.

Starting with a statement of the need for and qualities required in a communication audit, the handbook moves step by step through the various techniques of auditing up to the final report. At each stage the methodology is given practical reference by a fictionalized case study that unfolds in the form of an auditor's notebook. A sample communication audit report is based on that case study.

Thanks are due to the staff of the University of Calgary Communications Studies Program, especially Sylvia Mills; and to Marvin Abugov and Jack Bales of the Alberta Energy Resources Conservation Board for their encouragement and their splendid ideas about audits.

I would also like to acknowledge the inspiration and information I owe to Gerald Goldhaber's *Organizational Communication,* and *The ICA Audit*; Paul Hersey and Kenneth Blanchard for the use of their Situational Leadership diagram; Charles Redding for the concept of the 'double interact'; and Lawrence Kincaid for the convergence theory diagram.

S. C. Hamilton
Spring 1987

PART ONE

Introducing the Audit

Chapter 1
COMMUNICATION AUDITS

A communication audit is an objective report on the internal communication of an organization. The audit allows management to improve the way in which the organization deals with the information necessary to its operation.

■ WHY ORGANIZATIONS NEED COMMUNICATION AUDITS

Internal communication systems have never been more crucial to business success. The organization whose members do not interact effectively among themselves is neither efficient nor well-motivated. Accordingly, from time to time every business needs to examine its internal communication system and find out who is talking to whom, about what, through what channels and with what degree of success. By answering these questions, a communication audit provides the decision-making information that allows internal communication to be considerably improved and thereby enhances the organization's overall productivity. This has been shown to be so time and time again over the last few years.

A communication audit addresses the clarity, appropriateness and efficiency of internal organizational communications. Because it examines both formal and informal interactions, it can lead to improved morale and more successful motivation within the organization. A communication audit, however, is not a 'satisfaction study' designed to 'make the workers happier'; it is a practical assessment of information management and flow. Properly administered, it can help senior management coordinate all the many tasks and responsibilities necessary to fulfil the organization's goals.

Two analogies

A communication audit can be compared to a financial audit or to a medical check-up.

Financial audits discover whether an organization's money matters are in order. Cash flows are monitored, records checked and money management assessed by a professional accountant who then points out any omissions or transgressions in the organization's financial system. This process is a necessity in both law and business practice because of the number and complexity of economic transactions. In addition to the need to comply with standard business practice, a Chief Executive Officer (CEO) uses a financial audit as a management tool that allows him or her to improve efficiency. A periodic audit not only discovers errors and omissions, it also provides decision-making information that allows new plans to be made and fresh initiatives to be undertaken.

A regular medical check-up provides comparable information to each one of us as an individual. We ask our doctors to assess our overall health, hoping that we will be told that we are well, but knowing that it is better to be warned in advance before some disability or sickness becomes a serious threat to our well-being. We all need professional medical advice from time to time so that we can make intelligent decisions about exercise and diet as they affect our health. The doctor makes an analysis using specialized medical knowledge focused on our particular needs, but it is then up to the patient to take responsibility for continuing health by intelligently following the doctor's advice.

Likewise, a communication audit evaluates the 'health' of an organization's formal and informal information systems. Like the financial audit or the medical check-up, it points to deficiencies or problems, and recommends ways whereby the organization can function more smoothly and efficiently. It enhances the CEO's decision-making ability by ensuring that he or she knows more about the reality of the organization's communication functions and structure. As with the check-up, it is a specialized source of objective advice that should allow those in the organization responsible for communication to communicate more successfully. And who is responsible for communication in an organization? Every manager and ultimately the CEO.

■ FOCUSING A COMMUNICATION AUDIT

A communication audit examines the different ways in which people 'talk' to one another within an organization. It looks at:

- face-to-face communication, whether one-on-one or in groups;
- written communication in the form of letters, memos and internal reports;
- communication patterns among individuals, sections and departments;
- communication channels and frequency of interaction (communication work-load);
- communication content, its clarity and effectiveness;

- information needs of individuals, sections and departments;
- information technology, particularly with respect to the human and organizational aspects of using communication and information technology;
- informal communication, particularly as it affects motivation and performance;
- non-verbal communication (such as physical layout of work areas, marks of seniority or norms of dress and manner; as they affect the efficiency of the organization);
- communication climate, or 'corporate culture'.

The auditor uses the information gathered about the organization's current communication structure, frequency and content to assess the functions, roles and positions of personnel as they affect the flow of information necessary to the overall mission of the organization. Recommendations can then be made that:

- identify and correct information over- and under-load;
- adjust formal information flows to maximize efficiency;
- modify informal information flows to reinforce overall purposes;
- make intelligent use of existing information channels and technology;
- choose appropriate additional communication/information technology or systems.

An audit does not necessarily evaluate personnel, nor is it designed to pinpoint underproductive or negligent workers among the staff. An audit seeks to improve the communication effectiveness of interrelated business systems. Recommendations made are based on finding ways of maximizing communication efficiency by implementing appropriate adjustments to the system with the cooperation of those involved, rather than by radically changing the staff structure. This means that, to be successful, a communication audit must be marketed to employees as it actually is so that it will be built by a spirit of cooperation and mutual trust at all levels of the organization.

■ DECIDING WHEN TO PERFORM A COMMUNICATION AUDIT

An effective business needs systematic communication audits, just as it requires financial audits, management evaluations and other regular self-assessments. And this need is not limited to major corporations. Small businesses have information flow problems and to them the consequences are often more serious. Entrepreneurial businesses within major corporations, non-profit organizations, social and cultural organizations, and governmental agencies are similarly afflicted. Internal communication cannot be left to itself, because it is constantly modified by alterations in environment and by consequent internal changes in duties, responsibilities and roles. Accordingly, a communication audit should, like the financial audit, be a normal and regular part of management, rather than an emergency measure left until some pressing problem or difficulty arises.

Most organizations recognize that a communication audit is vital at times of change in the life of an organization, for example, when:

● major expansion is contemplated or enacted;
● a merger or business acquisition takes place;
● the organization must incrementally expand or reduce the number of personnel;
● new functions, product lines or corporate responsibilities are undertaken;
● circumstances beyond the organization's control change its context and function (as in the case of economic downturn or dramatic growth);
● planning to acquire new technology (especially if it is information- or communication-related).

Whether the next important move is to acquire new communication equipment or to alter the management structure, to initiate new product research or become involved in a merger, there is always a need for effective, productive communication, and it must be clear and unambiguous.

■ THE BENEFITS OF THE AUDIT

The primary benefit of a communication audit is that it leads to a deeper understanding of the internal communication structure and climate of the organization. From this flow a number of concrete and practical possibilities, including:

● improved productivity;
● more appropriate use of existing and future communications and information technology;
● more efficient use of time ;
● discovery of 'hidden' information resources;
● improved morale;
● a more vibrant corporate culture.

If the audit is carefully and clearly announced to employees as a non-punitive process with the goal of improving communications it becomes the hallmark of a confident management that is actively dedicated to improving the lot of employees. The staff, for their part, *once reassured*, will respond, encouraged by the simple fact that they are being consulted. Properly and efficiently administered, the audit builds on this confidence and optimism, seeking first to understand and then to improve the ways in which people communicate within the workplace.

The audit which heralds much and leads to naught will also speak volumes about a company's style and ability to react.

The sense that there is intrinsic worth to what is done in and by the organization cannot be manufactured by an audit, but it can be discovered and nurtured through the audit process and through the resultant implementation of changes that have the support of all the members of the organization.

Chapter 2
SELECTING AN AUDIT PROCESS

A CEO who is deciding whether to hold a communication audit will usually have some idea of what should appear in the final report. Such objectives are entirely valid, but it should be understood that an audit must not merely justify preconceived opinions, but rather should discover the actual state of communications before making adjustments to the way in which they take place. The CEO should be able to share opinions with the auditor, but rather as an individual contributor to the audit process than as a concealed power that manipulates its results. Therefore the first requirement from the audit is that it must be as professional and independent as the financial auditor's report that it partially resembles.

Once familiar with the process of the benefits that can flow from a communication audit, the CEO should seek a good 'match' between his or her expectations and the skills of the auditor. Every auditor has areas of special expertise, some being specifically able in surveys, focus groups or network analysis, over and above their competence in other methodologies. The CEO should take this into consideration in the light of the organization and its style of management. A large, bureaucratic organization will in all probability learn more from a 'content analysis' than a smaller, less formal organization which will probably need an audit that concentrates on interviews and 'focus groups'.

■ HOW LONG IT WILL TAKE AND WHAT IT WILL LOOK LIKE

There is no one single package of methodologies that can be applied in a communication audit to all organizations. It all depends on size, maturity, circumstances and budget. There is, however, a basic process that is dictated by concerns for quality of information and hence the reliability of recommendations and the effectiveness of their implementation. A 'quick and dirty' audit that produces only superficial changes to which few members of the organization are committed is counterproductive. Conversely, a drawn-out audit that takes months to prepare may well interfere with the day-to-day running of the organization to the point that its main goals and purposes are obscured, output declines and the organization's economic existence is compromised.

An audit will cost time and money, whoever undertakes it. On average, however, a fairly compact audit of an organization employing approximately 300 people ought to be handled in approximately a month. This presumes few time-consuming difficulties such as distant branch offices, interlocking companies or agencies, or problematic issues such as getting agreement from a number of unions.

Triangulation
Triangulation, or the simultaneous use of different, corroborating techniques (instruments), is the principle that controls all the approaches outlined in this handbook. No one methodology, be it surveys, interviews, focus groups, network or content analysis, is sufficient in itself. A single technique, even if rigorously administered, will produce biased results simply because of the inherent strengths and weaknesses in that methodology. By using triangulation, three simultaneously applied approaches tackle problems and opportunities from different perspectives, identifying issues by independent, corroborating evidence. It is just like finding your place on a map – with triangulation, your chances of being where you should be are much enhanced. This approach is not only efficient in terms of cost and time but of accuracy as well; showing facts from different angles not only corroborates but often stimulates solutions which go right to the heart of the matter. The report at the close of a triangulated audit is also likely to appeal to more people within the organization, hence generating a more widespread willingness to participate in implementation.

■ WHO SHOULD PERFORM A COMMUNICATION AUDIT

Having decided upon an audit, a CEO can make use of the services of either an external professional consultant, an internal communications specialist, or a team of in-house staff members.

Choosing a consultant
For many companies, an external professional consultant may well be the first and best choice. The reason is clear. They know what they are doing. They live on their skills and reputation. Outside consultants have:

● an absence of bias towards individuals within the organization;
● an independence of judgement;

- professional distance from the ongoing concerns and enthusiasms of the organization;
- potential for a relationship with the CEO based on equality and mutual respect;
- an absence of any real or perceived self-interest in the audit process.

Many senior managers will shake their heads at bringing in 'an outsider who won't understand the complexities of our business'. Before adopting that posture, consider the words of Peter Tidman who trained thousands of top business men to appear on TV: 'Every manager thinks his or her problems are unique, with very rare exceptions, they are not. The manager who cannot explain, ought not to be there.'

Choosing an in-house specialist
An organization can also consider using its internal communication specialist, especially one who is:

- autonomous within the organization (usually, this means reporting directly to the CEO);
- perceived by colleagues, superiors and subordinates as highly-qualified in his or her specialty;
- perceived as fair-minded and objective;
- newly-assigned or appointed.

In either of these two choices, the auditor must not only be *but also be perceived to be* an independent thinker whose activities will under no circumstances be interpreted as finding fault or conducting a purge on behalf of senior management. Clearly, both internal and external auditors may have this crucial qualification, on which rests the objectivity and effectiveness of the audit process. However, in many companies the communication function still does not come directly under the CEO, or the public relations or information officer does not give it its due. If the auditor is not an 'independent' then the audit will be seen as a power-play or worse, a cosmetic and low-priority exercise.

Choosing a team of in-house staff members
A third possibility may be suggested: have a management team made up of senior staff conduct the communication audit, making use of the techniques outlined in this handbook. Opposition to this approach which at first may seem both comprehensive and inexpensive is not merely to keep independent consultants in work. A committee is not usually an ideal source of responsible, objective assessment necessary for a good audit. The complexity of the audit process demands that one person be in charge not only of drawing together the data and

information, but also of presenting the eventual analysis and recommendations. A staff committee cannot negotiate effectively with the CEO without other personnel suspecting its motives that at its worst might undermine all authority within the organization. It is unlikely that a team of several colleagues within an organization can reach objective conclusions that are not biased (or at least appear to be biased) towards one or more individuals or departments. Finally, and most importantly, the auditor must have communication experience that cannot, as the CEO may at first believe, be picked up over a course of a lifetime of managing but rather is the result of training, study and appropriate period of apprenticeship in the field.

Combining abilities

The introduction of an audit into an organization not used to it causes anxieties. To alleviate this and obtain the best of both in and out of house resources and experience, the CEO may propose a team of (senior) staff members working alongside an outside professional auditor. During the fact finding phases the team know the workings of their organization best, and most importantly, they will 'own' any recommendations. The blueprint for change that has been objectively proposed by the auditor and CEO management team has the best chance of being implemented.

One advantage to a 'hand in glove' audit is to get it started down the right road from the beginning not only to ensure the appropriateness of the chosen audit process, but to keep in touch with reality. It does no good to an organization to be given a recommendation that it buy expensive communication equipment if money is not available to make such a purchase. If specific terms and conditions are set out at the contract negotiation stage, then the auditor can rise to the challenge of suggesting ingenious but practicable solutions appropriate to the organization. Under these circumstances, the auditor's recommendations are more likely to be implemented and the organization will benefit from the entire experience.

Regardless of how the organization proceeds, the auditor must be given the authority by the CEO to function autonomously and objectively. However, remember that if an auditor is left to 'get on with it', the CEO forfeits control and the auditor risks wasting time and money on dead ends and 'magical' solutions based on incorrect data.

If an audit is to be both comprehensive and comprehensible to the members of the organization, the initial contract must be negotiated to the satisfaction of both the CEO and the auditor, with its costs and benefits spelled out in advance. Specifically, they must agree about the appropriateness of the instruments proposed. It is legitimate for the CEO to declare certain areas (for example, details of corporate funding) 'off limits' to the auditor's scrutiny – provided any such limitations are agreed upon from the beginning. Equally, a conscientious consultant may declare from the first that some methods of enquiry may be inappropriate to a specific organization (for example, the organization's files may be too small for one audit method the 'content analysis' which relies on an extensive record of an organization's activities).

Having decided on an audit and who is best placed to carry it out, the next step is to set it up.

Chapter 3
SETTING UP
THE AUDIT PROCESS

■ OBTAINING A DETAILED BRIEF

The executive who is considering a communication audit should know what can legitimately be expected. This handbook offers him or her an opportunity to clarify exactly what the audit process entails and how it can benefit the organization. This chapter is dedicated to establishing a fair-minded agreement, and a subsequent effective relationship between CEO and auditor.

In what follows, it may seem that the route to a detailed brief is addressed from the perspective of the independent consultant and so covers the full range of techniques that may be adopted and outcomes that arise. It is of equal importance both to the in-house specialist and to the executive about to bring in an auditor.

■ INTRODUCING THE AUDIT

An auditor should prepare a prospectus or an information sheet that describes the services he or she has to offer and sets out what an audit is and how it can be used by the organization. The prospectus must strike a balance between the auditor's individual interests, skills and proficiencies, and the expected requirements of the particular organization. The effective auditor can here offer several coordinated techniques on the results of which clear analysis and useful recommendations can be made. The prospectus introduces an opportunity to set out those processes by which the CEO's needs will be met, and to initiate the relationship that will allow both parties to work together on the goal of improving communication within the organization.

Presenting a brief is perhaps best handled in a letter or memo to the CEO. The brief should itemize the various techniques and processes that the auditor offers, stipulating that not all are necessary or desirable in every case. In other words, the auditor should lay out the audit toolkit for inspection. A good brief outlines what is involved in the audit process, possible techniques and the general approach. It focuses on the audit as a means of enacting constructive change that must have the support of senior management both during the audit process and afterwards when implementing recommendations.

■ FIRST CONTACT

When the prospective auditor walks into the CEO's office (or the office of the contact person), he or she should already know exactly what can be achieved through the interview. The auditor would do well to find out tactfully whether or not the interviewer has the authority to purchase auditing services, and if not, how much influence he or she has on the final decision. The auditor should ensure that he or she meets the CEO as early as possible in the audit – it is vital that the person in authority makes a firm commitment from the beginning and remains fully aware of what is happening in the organization. The auditor should always bear in mind that there are a great number of reasons why someone might want to carry out an audit, not all of which are mutually beneficial. For example, the CEO may want to conduct some kind of vendetta using the auditor as its instigator. Equally the auditor may have a private motive for offering his services – an in-house specialist, for instance, may think of the audit exclusively as a means of raising his or her rank or salary.

Advice to the prospective auditor

If the auditor has to wait for a few minutes before the interview begins, this is the moment to record first impressions. Don't just disappear behind the daily paper or the magazines that are put in the waiting area, but instead take note of any such materials, the quality of the space and how visitors are treated. For the consultant auditor this is the first and only chance to experience how it feels to be a newcomer to the organization, and perceptions should not slide by unrecorded. The in-house auditor, too, may use these moments to look at the organization from a new angle. Similarly, when the interview is over, the auditor should capture any other impressions on paper.

The auditor's principal requirement from the interview is to know that he or she is taking positive steps towards an agreement that will benefit both parties. This should be made very clear to the CEO or contact person and will focus the entire discussion.

It is sometimes possible for the auditor to note down those expectations as the interview goes on. This will be useful at the close of the interview when the auditor will be in a position to look back on notes and modify them into some such statement as: 'If I understand you correctly, you need an internal communication audit that would incorporate an employee survey, a network analysis and an examination of your internal memos and correspondence. You'd also like me to offer suggestions about how you could use existing technology better, and what equipment should be added.' When the auditor has restated this understanding, the two parties can begin to reach an agreement.

Advice to the organization

The CEO or contact person (who is often the communications officer) should use the interview not only to establish the auditor's technical qualifications, but also to evaluate how effectively he or she communicates them. Eventually, the auditor will set out results and recommendations in a final report and presentation, and if these final products are to be effectively translated into action, they must be lucidly and specifically expressed. The auditor's prospectus should have made clear what he or she can do in general terms: the interview serves to find out how the audit can be tailored to the needs of the particular organization.

There is a balance between on the one hand, giving the auditor *carte blanche*, and thereby abdicating responsibility; and on the other, limiting the audit by stressing only those concerns that preoccupy the organization at that moment. The audit process both can and should turn up problems and opportunities that are *not* apparent before it begins; what the CEO needs to know is that this will be done in an objective and disciplined fashion. The ideal relationship is one based on mutual, professional respect, which implies that the CEO should be confident that the auditor can fulfil plans involving time and budget with a responsible awareness of contingencies that will inevitably cause minor alterations to scheduling. Be wary of the consultant who appears to have an ironclad and inflexible approach to the audit process.

Avoid giving a detailed history of the organization and its problems at the first meeting. At a later interview it is possible to flesh out the details of concerns and issues: for the present, it is the audit process that is at issue, its instruments or methods, timetable, costs and benefits.

Advice to beginners

An auditor beginning a career in communication or a member of in-house personnel who is taking on this new responsibility may be tempted to disclose and apologize for inexperience, and perhaps even to offer a cut rate or accept a ludicrously low budget. Such temptations must be resisted as they undermine the credibility both of the auditor and of the audit itself. They also invite an unequal relationship wherein the auditor is the inferior. Lack of confidence on the part of the auditor denigrates the skills and abilities that he or she is trying to put to work, and makes it less likely that the CEO will accept and act upon the final report.

A checklist

To confirm any agreements reached during the interview it is important that the auditor afterwards restates all progress made. This can be done by letter from an outside consultant or by memo from an internal specialist. The auditor should here thank the CEO for the interview and recapitulate what was discussed and what should happen next. He or she should also, of course, provide any further information which may have been requested.

This form of reminder allows both parties to review the interview and have a clear understanding of the audit process and how it can best be applied to the particular organization.

■ THE CONTRACT OR THE JOB DESCRIPTION

The audit contract, or, in the case of an inside auditor, the job description, should state exactly what the auditor will do and what the organization will do to make the job possible. In addition to overall agreement on the conduct and focus of the audit, both parties – particularly when an outside consultant is involved – should be clear on such practical matters as:

- Who pays for the stamps, if a questionnaire is sent out?
- Who does the typing, printing, folding and stuffing of questionnaires?
- How much time will interviews with employees take up?
- Will the auditor take all work home, or (preferably) will the organization supply office space?
- What secretarial services will the organization supply?
- Who does any computer data entry and manipulation, where, and at what cost?

There is no one correct answer to any of these questions, but there must be explicit agreement, or the consultant auditor may find that profits are being eaten up paying for items such as stamps and printing because the responsibility was not made clear in the contract. Conversely, the organization must not be disrupted by unreasonable claims on time and resources that were not foreseen from the first.

Cost and time

Most important, both parties must be willing to talk about time and money. The consultant auditor should know in advance how much his or her services cost, how payment should be made, and approximately how long the process will take. An in-house specialist should make sure that a budget sufficient to cover all costs is specified for the audit and that work schedules are so arranged that neither the audit nor any other duties he or she regularly performs are neglected. The CEO should be prepared to authorize a reasonable expenditure both in terms of budget and commitment of organizational time. That means, both sides must have addressed certain questions before any detailed job description is drawn up or before a contract is made.

The consultant auditor must decide on an hourly or daily rate of pay for his or her services, or be ready to propose a total figure for the completed contract. Extra expenses should also be allowed for. The CEO must know what kind of resources the organization can offer in terms of accommodation, secretarial help, etc. He or she must also work out how much time can be committed to the audit and accordingly reschedule the work of personnel who are affected. The two parties must agree on fixed deadlines and on check-points at which it can be clearly established that the project is on time and on budget.

If both sides are forthright at the outset about these issues, they will communicate clearly and thereby set an example not only for the audit but for its implementation. If they are too flexible and accommodating, they can find themselves with a contract in which both lose money and credibility as a result of extra expenses over which they have no control. Moreover, in the auditor's case, he or she will have established himself as a poor communicator, and any experienced executive will be unlikely to have faith in his or her work.

Drawing up the document

Now let us assume that all these hurdles have been cleared and both the CEO and the auditor are willing to go ahead and make a formal agreement. This need not be any more than an exchange of letters or memos, but it does require that both sides commit to paper and have agreement in writing on exactly what it is that will be done with, for and to the organization. The agreement must clearly state the following conditions:

- how much will be charged or budgeted;
- when and how payments to a consultant auditor are to be made;
- what expenses are to be paid by whom;
- when the deadlines are for interim and final reports;
- how many copies of the final report are needed.

■ INTRODUCING THE CASE STUDY

There follows the first instalment of the handbook's fictionalized case study. A consultant auditor has been commissioned by a large organization to investigate existing communication flows and recommend improvements. The procedures followed and the notes kept by this auditor illustrate how the handbook's guidelines can be put into effect by both in-house and external specialists.

First contact

I made it! Contact with Regal Instruments! I looked at the register of companies and checked advertising in trade magazines. I'm dealing with a company that claims to be a leading producer of professional tools used in heavy equipment industries. It was founded fifteen years ago, and is privately owned. Three years ago it expanded into new quarters in an industrial park on the edge of the city. The building was constructed expressly for Regal, and was celebrated at the time of opening in the business pages of the daily papers.

My first interview was with Shelley Peters, the Communications Officer, who told me that she has just been promoted. The President and CEO, J. B. King, has recently taken the initiative to 'improve communications', and has given Ms Peters the task of coordinating this effort under his direction.

I think I established a good rapport with Shelley.

Notes and comments

Shelley Peters, Communications Officer. Five years experience with large firms as technical writer, editor of staff magazine. Three years with Regal. She is part of the Marketing Division and responsible for a variety of tasks including producing the newsletter, and public relations, but has no authority or funding to improve them. According to her, King recently attended a conference on communications in business and was converted. He has acquired word processing equipment for the firm, is considering electronic messaging, wonders whether his company is ready for the changes. Shelley suggested an audit to find out the state of affairs, and to provide a benchmark. He was all for it.

The building is attractively landscaped, designed. Inside, much use of indoor plants as screens. First floor is huge: includes manufacturing space. Four storey office tower rises above, two departments to a floor, executive level on top. Pastel tones. More plants . . . like a jungle! A person who looked like a senior secretary in front of a hedge of little fig trees pointed out waiting area. Recent business magazines, trades, on display on low glass coffee-table. No coffee. Six photos on wall of J. B. King being presented awards for export, excellence of product, etc. No clue here as to what it is they make!

Nobody but a secretary came past during ten minute wait. Is this a holiday? Or do people not visit the top floor?

S. P. seems over-anxious to please. Why?

PART TWO
Conducting a Successful Audit

Chapter 4
THE WALK-AROUND AND THE ACTION PLAN

Once the need for a communication audit has been recognized and the most suitable process selected, the auditor can begin a detailed study of the organization, its strengths and weaknesses. Part Two examines the different 'instruments' or techniques open to the auditor, from 'focus group' meetings and staff surveys to an in-depth 'network analysis.'

■ THE PASSPORT LETTER

The first step is to inform all members of the organization that a communication audit is to be conducted, to describe the auditor's role and the procedures that will be followed during the audit.

If there are different offices, locations, a union representative or separate sub-sections within the organization, this can be achieved by circulating a brief 'passport letter'. This will be signed by the CEO and will explain why the audit is necessary and how it will be carried out. It will also provide assurance that although the auditor may be new to the company, he or she has not been employed purely to seek out people who can be fired. It is a good idea for the auditor to write this letter in draft for the CEO to sign, and then have it sent by him or her to all the members of the organization. A copy of the letter should be retained to show to people who may have forgotten its contents when the auditor visits them later in the project. A reasonable format for this letter is illustrated in Fig. 4.1 where Pat Smith, the consultant auditor in the handbook's case study, has been appointed to conduct an audit.

■ THE WALK-AROUND

The next step in any communication audit is the 'walk-around'. This is of obvious importance for external consultants, but internal auditors will also find it a valuable opportunity to view the organization as a whole and to inform employees of the objectives of the audit.

The walk-around is neither a social event, nor the beginning of structured analysis. However, it is an important step in getting to know the members of the organization. It also gives the auditor an opportunity to make preliminary plans and intuitive assessments.

The Chief Executive Officer
The walk-around should include an interview with the CEO. This may well be the last chance for the auditor to talk with him or her before the audit starts in earnest.

The employees
During the walk-around employees should be given a clear idea of who the auditor is and what he or she is doing. The auditor should be prepared to summarize what is going to be done and how this will affect the organization, neither going into great detail, nor allowing anyone to brush over the role.

President's Office
Regal Instruments

To all staff

Pat Smith will be working within Regal from January to March. Pat will be conducting a communication audit of the company in order that we may improve our overall efficiency in written, spoken and other forms of communication.

Pat Smith will be calling upon the members of Regal to complete forms and questionnaires, or to participate in interviews or focus group meetings. All questionnaires and discussions will be held in confidence by Pat, and members of Regal are encouraged to answer questions frankly. Questionnaires will be brief, taking no more than 15 minutes to complete. Interviews and focus group meetings will be scheduled by Pat with the approval of departmental supervisors to ensure minimal disruption of normal work patterns.

Regal Instruments already has a high standard of internal communication, but we can do better – especially since we both have and are contemplating acquiring new communication equipment. In order to make the best use of all our resources, both human and mechanical, Regal has secured the services of Pat Smith.

I wish to make it clear to all members of Regal Instruments that this communication audit is a means of improving the way that we do business, and no member of our firm need feel in any way threatened by the process. Pat Smith is making an objective assessment, the results of which will be a better and more efficient working environment for us all.

Pat will be based in the office of Ms Peters.

J. B. King, President, Regal Instruments

Figure 4.1 A sample passport letter

What to look for

The auditor will gain many new impressions during the walk-around. The following checklist will ensure nothing important is missed.

How do people address each other?
With titles? First names? Formally or informally?
Where do you detect differences that might be indicative of us-them behaviour between departments, senior and junior management, executives and workers?

What clues are there to status or job?
Conventional clothing or uniforms? Office arrangements? Evidence of 'perks' such as exclusive relaxation areas, parking, cafeterias, etc?

Where do people congregate to speak?
Is business done in closed offices? Do people chat in the halls? Do they conduct meetings there? Is there a staff room or other social area? How is it used?

How is formal communication made?
Are there notice boards, in-out boards, timetables? Is there a rule-book or policy manual visible? Is there a company phone book or list? Is there any kind of crisis manual or suggestion box? Are such things actually used, or are they merely for show?

How are people and offices arranged?
Does senior management share the top floor? Are there buffers to accessing senior management? What are they? If the office is open plan, are some areas more desirable than others? Do supervisors have offices? How do they use them?

Are there visible staff motivation efforts?
Posters, sign up lists for recreational activities?

In addition, the auditor should note the following.

- Ask people what they do, even if the guide for the walk-around summarizes each person's responsibility. Note down how responsibilities are described both by the guide and by the individual workers – there may well be differences that go beyond words, and the words themselves may be clues to communication problems or opportunities.
- Be attentive to everyone: do not be deflected by rank. Different opinions will be needed to check out whether indeed, 'We're all one big happy family here,' as a manager may say.

● Take time between meetings to write down in a notebook at least the titles and names of those to whom you are introduced; and if possible, a few words that will recall the conversation. Needless to say, these notes are private.

Not everyone will be equally pleased to see the auditor or equally willing to cooperate. If forewarned, the auditor can politely tell the over-enthusiastic to wait and seek a more opportune time, approach withdrawn individuals, and minimize rumours about the supposed 'real purpose' of the audit by consistently telling the same story to everyone.

Intuition in the audit process

When the auditor first walks around a business, some aspects of communication will strike him or her immediately at an intuitive level. For example, the auditor may feel comfortable, uncomfortable, welcomed, faced by hostility, accepted as a contributor, suspected as an interfering busybody, invited to join in a group effort or rejected as a foreigner.

Overall, assessment of the walk-around may tip towards the positive or the negative. One thing is sure — it will always be mixed. That first sense of acceptance or rejection is worth attending to, and it definitely should be recorded, but it is an imperfect guide to what will follow. It is compounded more of feelings than thoughts, and feelings are short lived. The auditor will be stimulated by matters of the moment that may well be the product of mood, the moods of others and a host of other circumstances.

Nonetheless, when all these sources of possible mistakes are taken into consideration, the intuitive reaction to the organization is important. First of all, it affects the attitude the auditor will take to the job, and thus is something that must be managed consciously. Second, it is quite possible that the auditor has, in an intuitive flash, zeroed in on core problems and possibilities that can be guides during the mechanics of auditing the organization.

No questionnaire can tell what is perceived when someone walks in the door and is confronted by a barrier of desks and countertops, a receptionist who is trying to answer the phone and type at the same time, a CEO who lurks behind a closed door. All these are examples of non-verbal communication that are accepted unquestioningly by permanent staff but that a sensitive, observant auditor may discover.

Impressions are therefore important and should be noted down, but not analyzed. That comes later. Intuitions may help narrow the focus of the audit, but should not circumscribe its methodology. The auditor must during the course of the audit make objective what is at this point a subjective intuition, otherwise he or she will never be able to communicate impressions to those able to make changes.

The various instruments described in this book do not exist simply to justify intuitions. They will also generate information which could never be discovered simply by walking around and observing the ways in which staff communicate. For example, only by asking everyone in a series of interviews or surveys can the auditor discover that some (and which) of the people in the organization are profoundly unhappy about the benefits package, that some (and which) are unaware of key elements of company policy, that some believe they know about a 'mission statement' or company objective that has never been written down or formally announced in clear, unambiguous terms. Such issues are the stuff of analytical methodologies.

The notebook

The notebook in which the auditor jots down impressions is a most vital tool at this stage of the audit. Without notes, the auditor will never know whether he or she is driven by a mistaken first impression, or whether initial assessment was right, despite all that was later told.

A final word of caution

The auditor should remember that the organization may well be different from the one in which he or she would like to work, and yet be an entirely viable way of conducting business. In other words, it is important not to allow perceptions and wishes to rule thinking.

■ THE ACTION PLAN

The action plan is essentially a critical path that ends with the formal presentation of the report. The auditor should start at this final point and reason backwards to the present. At all costs, the project should not be started without a plan.

Drawing up a plan

The auditor should proceed as follows:

- On a calendar, mark in as accurately as possible the day the final report is due. If there is no specific day that can be predicted, then draw a heavy red line around the earliest and latest days, and choose the most convenient date as the working hypothesis.
- Plot in the holidays, days off and days when the organization is very busy with some regular but not routine functions, such as annual stocktaking.

- Examine the number of real working days, as opposed to time elapsed or apparent working days. This exercise may well yield at least one minor shock.
- Mark in time for the preparation of the report. If it is to be printed in more than two copies, allow ample time for this – time may have to be booked in advance in order to fit into a printer's schedule.
- Work backwards towards the present, allowing proofing time, editing time, revising time, writing time, interim report discussion with the CEO and most of all, thinking time.

At the end of this process, the auditor will have a date by which data collection and analysis must be complete. It is important to remember to leave time for data processing, and to remember that tasks such as keying in figures are the source of many time-consuming hitches and problems. A computer crash only happens in the last stages of data entry, and the more urgent the task or the later at night it gets, the more likely it is that someone will inadvertently push the global delete button or otherwise mislay valuable data.

What time remains will seem very short indeed. Into it the auditor must fit surveys, interviews, network and content analysis and other information-gathering techniques, allowing time for the filling-in and returning of questionnaires, rescheduling of interviews and focus groups. Advance warning should be given if the auditor wishes to examine documents or meet key people – such as vice presidents who may be unavailable, or union workers who must have permission from a shop steward.

Several time-saving techniques can be employed. By careful scheduling periods of heavy activity within the organization can be avoided. Different activities can be arranged to take place simultaneously, by delegating responsibility and also by working 'within the cracks' caused by the time taken completing and processing questionnaires. The auditor can telephone staff to encourage them to complete questionnaires, and drop off spots convenient for employees can be provided for their speedy return.

There is no perfect method of sequencing activities. It can be argued that better results will be obtained from a focus group if the data from a questionnaire is already available, and conversely, that the auditor will ask more suitable questions if the focus group has been conducted first. Contingencies, plus internal advice, plus the initial assessment during the walk-around will dictate the best order.

Scheduling the work of others
If working in a team, or with assistants, typists, data processors or other helpers, the auditor should plot not only when key staff are

needed, but also their availability so that last-minute panics can be avoided. If the organization has agreed to provide secretarial or other assistance, the auditor should not expect audit work to be given high priority. If the CEO urgently needs extra help audit work is most likely to get 'bumped', because it is not a part of the usual office load. Though the auditor will learn about the power structure of the organization from such an event, there are less frustrating ways of acquiring the same information.

Discussing the action plan

The action plan should be drafted and if conducted by an external auditor should be discussed in detail with the internal contact. He or she may have both good and bad news in that there may be more holidays than bargained for, executives may be away, or there may be non-standard work weeks when the organization goes through some internal upheaval. On the other hand, the contact person may be willing to make accommodations, offer useful suggestions or find alternative routes to the goal. A typical action plan is shown in Table 4.1 where the different stages of the action plan are set out in parallel activity 'tracks'.

The auditor will find it helpful to have a personal version of the action plan in the form of a notice-board with room for names of interviewees, availability times of technicians, etc. It must be up to date and accurate, because it will be the controlling factor in the auditor's life for the duration of the project. If it hangs in some prominent place, the auditor can add to it, check things off on it, remind him or herself of details, and keep on target.

■ THE CASE STUDY CONTINUES

Jan. 12 Walk-around

This is a hierarchy. All the leaders are on the top floor. It's as simple as that. Cafeteria in basement, very much for the workers. Management goes out to lunch. I saw several staff eating their lunches at their desks. Top floor is President, two Vice Presidents (who weren't there), secretary, receptionist, conference room, spare office (which will be mine for the duration), another conference room.

Next floor down holds Accounting and Marketing. Next comes Sales and Transportation, then Design has a floor to itself, finally at ground floor Production and Maintenance are squashed between the display area at the entrance and the factory, which takes up a huge adjunct to the offices, much longer and bigger than they are tall.

The potted palm jungle on the top floor gets thinner and thinner the lower

Date Day	Track one	Track two	Track three
12 Jan M	Walk around		
13 Tu	**Action plan**	**Set up focus group**	
14 W	Draft questionnaires		
15 Th	**Approve survey**	Focus meeting	
16 F	Revise, print questionnaires	Set up content analysis	
17 Sa	Write up meeting		
19 M	Hand out questionnaires	**Plan interviews**	*Content Analysis*
20 Tu	Interviews		*Content Analysis*
21 W	Deadline for questionnaires	Interviews	*Data entry of questionnaires*
22 Th	Interviews		*Data entry of questionnaires*
23 F	**Plan network analysis day**		Check data, *process*
24 Sa	*Print network analysis forms*	Write up interviews	*Process*
26 M	N-day		
27 Tu	Analyze network analysis forms	Technology assessment	*Data entry of network analysis data*
28 W	Analyze data and begin writing report	*Type or word process report*	
29 Th	Continue analyzing data and writing report	*Type or word process report*	
30 F	**Present interim report**		
31 Sa	Revise, complete and design graphs for final report		
2 Feb M	Write, edit report	*Type or word process report*	*Computerize graphs*
3 Tu	Edit and proofread report		
4 W	Check, copy, collate, bind, make overheads, check availability of presentation room		
5 Th	Rehearse presentation		
6 F	Present final report		

Italics = delegated   **Bold** = carried out with contact person

Table 4.1 A sample action plan

down the building you go. So do the carpets. However, everyone seems to have the same kind of unit-desk, except of course for the President and VPs, who have great huge slabs of polished wood.

Top floor is open plan jungle with secretaries and receptionist lurking in the bushes, and the President and VPs behind huge panelled oak doors. Other floors are identical in layout: open plan with corner offices for the managers, carefully arranged so that they are at diagonals from each other. The other corners are meeting rooms. Each floor is mathematically divided in two and each department has the same floor area to work with, which is absurd, since Accounting has nine staff, and Sales and Marketing seven and three respectively. The shoulder high screens make bee-hive sections, each cell containing a person.

The Production department is virtually part of the plant. A quick walk-around of the shop floor told me very little. It's clean, modern, the workers are obviously highly skilled, using very modern equipment including one computerized robot. Workers are mostly in their thirties, with a few older men. Fifteen women, all but three doing fine assembly work. Manager from Design was there. She's a woman, about 35, and she was talking with a man of about 55. They were holding a highly-technical discussion about a new piece of equipment, and there was obvious mutual respect in the way they interacted.

Accounting is one of the larger sections with nine people in all. Marketing has only four (of which Communication – Shelley – is one), but they still have a half-floor like the other sections. Sales looks like a warehouse of samples and sales kits with a secretary. Transportation is like Accounting, but the floor arrangement is different: the bee-hive is clustered around the Manager's office but he doesn't even seem to use it.

Everyone was working, some feverishly, some doggedly. Visiting among the cubicles seems to be the norm, rather than phone calls. I tended to meet people who were conferring in pairs, and they were working discussions, not social chats.

Managers get 'mistered', everyone else goes by first names, although there are little name-plates beside their cubicles giving both name and title. Secretaries don't have last names. They have little plastic signs on their desks saying 'Debbie' and 'Cathie' and 'Betty'.

Inexplicably, Shelley is working amid Marketing. In it, but not counted in it: one of those anomalies. I'd like to know who worked out the allocation of space: it's totally conceptual. Shelley gave me an organization chart after she'd shown me around. It's a fascinating contradiction to the hierarchical arrangement: officially, this is a flat organization!

Dramatis personae

Accounting
Ben Wills. Late 50s. Grey suit. Half-glasses. Serious speech handicap. Must reserve judgement here; it doesn't seem to interfere with what he does.

Design
Lisa Fremden. Late 30s. Degrees on office wall from three countries. Grasped principle of audit immediately. Very efficient.

Sales
Michael Worsley. 40s? Rumpled and harried, a pair of half-glasses on the end of his nose. No time to talk.

Marketing
Daniel Scanlon. 30s. Upwardly mobile in a blue suit. Problem here? Could try to take over the process?

Transportation
Joe Bailey. A white shock of hair that stands on end, in complete contradiction to his imperturbable manner. He's very pleasant and completely in charge. While we talked, he answered questions from three different people (all women in his department). Knew everything. Had time to smile and make jokes. (First sense of humour discovered today.)

Production
C. Franks. Definitely 'mister'. No informality here. Clipboard in hand. (Is he trying to look older/wiser/more in control than he actually is?) He could be any age.

Maintenance
So far only a name on the door. P. Shaughnessey. Not at home. Smallest office of anyone – literally a cupboard under the stairs. Shelley told me that he is a nocturnal creature, along with his staff.

CEO's secretary
Ethel Walters. Iron grey hair in a bun. Twin-sets. Desk strategically inhabited by symmetrical piles of paper. Ordered her typist to retype two letters. The woman visibly cringed. EW definitely a power to be reckoned with.

Receptionist, 5th Floor
Carol Manning. 20s. Decorative. Soft voiced.

The CEO
J. B. King. Early 50s, lean, balding, but tanned on top. Very direct style: fixes you with grey-blue eyes, talks constantly about 'What we're going to do . . .' VERY proud of his building. Didn't hide behind his desk, but sat in window with light behind him and against me, so that he could watch me and I had to squint. It wasn't severe, in fact I don't even think it was deliberate, but it worked.

I couldn't 'read' him, so I covertly itemized his office instead. It's a showplace where he spends his leisure as well as working time. Rugs on the floor. Non-office furniture such as a sofa, obviously chosen by him. It's under a big painting of a Coast Guard boat (ship?) in heavy sea (I wonder why?).

He wonders out loud, 'Will they (the staff) be up to what's going to happen in the next five years?' and I thought he was about to give me some clue as to what he had in mind. He said 'Not everyone will make it. The 21st century's coming a few years early at Regal.' I told him that in my view an audit is not a way of finding out who to fire, and he stopped to think that one through, then agreed. (Watch this carefully??)

If the way he approved Shelley's proposal about me and the audit is any indication, he trusts his managers. Reads the top page with great care, skims the rest. (Remember to write a good executive summary to my report!) After that, it was a rehash of our first meeting, only with dates and times. Then the phone rang, and he excused himself.

Action plan

Shelley promises me a temporary employee as my secretary, which is much better than I expected. She 'will try' to get a word processor terminal into my office. She was surprised that I'd want to have my secretary in there with me. After she left, I realized that she was unconsciously telling me about the great gulf between secretaries and staff – I was right about their lack of last names being a status symbol.

Chapter 5
FOCUS GROUPS

A focus group is a selection of members of an organization who are interviewed as a group by the communication auditor. Where surveys and network analysis take a snapshot of a slice of the organization at a particular time (*see:* Chapters 6 and 7), focus groups involve the auditor in the organization's history, hopes, fears, and all its human dynamics. Though the methodology is not comparable in terms of accuracy to the mechanical process of statistically analyzing forms, nonetheless it is one of the richest and most telling ways not only of understanding the organization but also of finding ways of improving it.

The focus group is a tool in the auditing process. It not only discovers problems, but can assist in curing them. If abused or clumsily managed, it can also create problems and destroy potential within the audit process.

Focus groups are at the intersection of intuitive and analytical, subjective and objective. The auditor is thus most deeply involved and yet most in need of the ability to maintain objectivity.

■ SELECTION OF THE GROUP

The auditor is looking for a cross-section of the organization with respect to position and status. It is important to have people who will talk, interact, and be forthright; but not people who merely talk a lot.

Generally speaking, the auditor wants opinion leaders, who will not necessarily be the people nominally in charge. A full-scale network analysis (*see:* Chapter 7) will identify such people as 'nodes' or focus points of interaction; however, even without this, it is usually possible to identify people intuitively with considerable accuracy. (It is important that the auditor be able to 'handle' the people, thus something about them should be known before the meeting.)

The members
Experience and research have shown that from five to seven people constitute the most effective focus group. In addition to the partici-

pants, there should be the auditor as moderator, and a person to record the meeting who is totally neutral.

The list should be balanced male-female in the same proportions as the organization. In the case of a male-dominated institution, it should have more than one woman, even if this is not mathematically justifiable. The appearance of a 'token' woman should be avoided. The group should include:

- a senior executive (*not* the CEO);
- a secretary or receptionist;
- a mid-rank managerial person;
- a technician or person whose contribution to the organization is primarily with his/her hands and skills;
- in the case of a factory operation, at least one or (preferably) two 'workers';
- in the case of a bureaucracy, one or two junior people;
- in the case of a non-profit, charitable or social-issue organization, at least one 'client' and at least one 'field worker';
- in the case of an organization with a board of directors, one person from this board (*not* the senior executive/president/chairman).

In short, all the constituent parts of the organization should be represented by people *other than* the nominal or formal leaders, save insofar as they are themselves representative of their group (a director of the directors, a manager of all managers, a supervisor of all supervisors). Some pains should be taken to ensure that there is a fair distribution across the varying sections of the organization.

The final result should be a group wherein people not only represent their sections or work-areas, but also their status levels across the firm. This ensures that each person 'wears two hats', and thus is less likely to become involved in defending his or her job, section or sub-section.

The venue

It is important that the group is not disturbed for the half-day allotted to the process. The room should be comfortable, well-lit, equipped with coffee, tea, soft drinks and snacks, have a blackboard, and be arranged in such a way as to create a round-table atmosphere wherein nobody confronts anyone else. What people should see when they first enter are coffee, tea or juice, so that their first act together is to share refreshments and relax. Under no conditions should a boardroom table be set up where people face each other and can take physical sides in order to act out the intellectual or emotional sides they were on before they entered the room.

A tape recorder is *not* a good idea for focus group meetings. Not only can it be threatening, it is not particularly useful, in that it is the joint agreement reached during the meeting that is at issue, not the individual steps towards (and sometimes away from) a resolution.

■ THE MEETING

Breaking the ice

When everyone is sitting comfortably, the auditor should begin with a small, non-threatening self-discovery exercise, and hand out a questionnaire, such as the TRO questionnaire illustrated in Fig. 5.1. (T=task, R=relationship and O=organization.)

By taking a cross-section of an organization such as the focus group and averaging scores that give perceptions of that organization, it is possible to gain a more objective idea of the 'style' or 'climate' of the organization. The auditor may want to invite the group to see how members 'fit' against an averaged perception. Alternatively, the forms can be collected and analyzed later. This decision should be made on intuitions about how comfortable people are with the situation. This exercise is used to create a sense of participation as well as to get information, so it is important that the operation and the discussion that will follow are not allowed to become threatening.

The auditor should not take more than half an hour with the questionnaire.

Formulating the problem

This is where the meeting will start to give concrete, specific information. If a positive atmosphere has been created, people should be willing to work together with the auditor as moderator.

The auditor should set the group a problem: the formulation of a mission statement (company objective) for the firm. This can be expressed by saying that the existing mission statement is not clear, or (and this is probably the more likely) that there is *no* clear mission statement, and that the group should help formulate one based on their understanding of what the organization is and does. This is an impossible task to complete in three hours. It takes on average six months to write a mission statement for a firm, if the process is done with full input by all concerned. However, it is possible for the representative members of a focus group to create an adequate first draft that can be a useful document for both the auditor and the management of the firm.

At this point, the auditor should reassure people that everything taking place in the focus group, particularly their opinions and points

TRO QUESTIONNAIRE

On the LEFT, register your agreement or disagreement on a scale of 1 to 5 with the values expressed by the following statements.

On the RIGHT, using the same 1 – 5 scale, register how you feel your organization perceives these values.

My score	**Scale** (Disagree) 1 2 3 4 5 (Agree)	**Organization score**
☐	a) Motivation is the key to performance	☐
☐	b) The job isn't finished until the paperwork is done	☐
☐	c) Pride in quality of service and product creates excellence	☐
☐	d) Harmonious interaction among workmates is necessary and desirable	☐
☐	e) Without accurate record-keeping, there can be no informed decisions	☐
☐	f) Consistency of product and service determines economic success	☐
☐	g) Creative interaction implies both conflict and the resolution of that conflict	☐
☐	h) People need framework, system and structure	☐
☐	i) Clarity, consistency and objectivity are the characteristics of effective orders	☐
☐	j) Positive reinforcement is more effective than fault-finding	☐
☐	k) Good housekeeping is essential to any organization	☐
☐	l) In the last analysis, what is made and done is more important than how it is achieved	☐
☐	m) Innovation usually starts with an innovator or a misfit who does not follow policy	☐
☐	n) Seniority is an important determinant in promotion	☐
☐	o) For every task, there is a right way of doing it	☐
☐	p) Empathy, honesty and trust are essential to effective interaction	☐
☐	q) The chain of command anchors an organization to precedent and procedure	☐
☐	r) To work effectively together, it is only necessary that people know what they must do.	☐

Continued over

Figure 5.1 A Task/Relationship/Organization questionnaire

continued

TRO SCORE SHEET

Taking the numbers from BOTH right and left columns on your questionnaire and add together the following groups:

My score	Organiza- tion score	My score	Organiza- tion score	My score	Organiza- tion score
a ☐	☐	b ☐	☐	c ☐	☐
d ☐	☐	e ☐	☐	f ☐	☐
g ☐	☐	h ☐	☐	i ☐	☐
j ☐	☐	k ☐	☐	l ☐	☐
m ☐	☐	n ☐	☐	o ☐	☐
p ☐	☐	q ☐	☐	r ☐	☐

Now add each of the above columns

☐	☐	☐	☐	☐	☐

Now divide each of the above totals by 6 to obtain an average

☐	☐	☐	☐	☐	☐
Me	Organization	Me	Organization	Me	Organization
RELATIONSHIP		**ORGANIZATION**		**TASK**	

Now plot your scores by circling the appropriate numbers on the Y-diagram below, and the organization's scores by making a box around the appropriate numbers on the diagram. Now join the circles and the boxes with straight lines to form two (overlapping) triangles.

RELATIONSHIP

5

4

3

2

1

2　　2

3　　　3

4　　　　4

5　　　　　5

TASK　　　　**ORGANIZATION**

continued over

continued

Interpreting the TRO Y-diagram

Relationship: scores the concern for human interaction of people as people, ie: interpersonal warmth or coldness.
Task: scores the concern for production, in terms of physical, measurable output.
Organization: scores the concern for the administrative function within the organization.

There are no 'right answers' to the TRO questionnaire. There is, however, a better or worse 'fit' between you and your organization. If you perceive the organization as being very task and organization biased (for example, a R 2, T 5, O 5 triangle), while you see yourself as being more geared towards relationships (for example, a R 5, T 3, O 1 triangle) then you are at odds with your organization, and you probably are experiencing a certain amount of distress. If your triangle overlaps with the organization's triangle as you perceive it, then you probably find yourself interpreting any stress you feel as a challenge.

Figure 5.1 A Task/Relationship/Organization questionnaire

of view, will be respected as confidential. Any person present as a minute-taker or recorder should be introduced and it should be explained that he or she is there to act as scribe, recorder, and group memory, and that his or her notes will all be kept absolutely private.

It is useful to hand people an explanation of what a mission statement is and what goes into it. Figure 5.2 is a useful guide.

Mission statement

Definition An expression of the basic purpose of the organization or organizational unit

Criteria

    1 States the purpose or main thrust of the organization
    2 Indicates a product or service
    3 Mentions a technology or approach
    4 Outlines the market it serves
    5 Mentions constraints such as acts, laws or charters

Figure 5.2 A sample mission statement

The auditor should then proceed as follows: (a) allow the group to study the explanation briefly, but not long enough to 'set their own ideas in stone'; (b) address the meeting as a group and ask the question as simply as possible, such as 'What does this organization do?'; and (c) allow everyone to speak, but only briefly. A round-robin set of contributions from each person should follow. The recorder should summarize responses on the blackboard as people speak so that the notes can be easily read. If people try to explain, justify, point to authority, or claim special position, they should be politely inter-rupted, and persuaded that this first round is to collect first impressions and perceptions – nobody is 'right' at this stage of the game. Similarly, anyone who pulls rank or starts sentences such as 'Surely you people in sales know that . . .' should be neutralized quickly by reminding the group that at this point the objective is to find out what the organization is and presently does, *not* what it *ought to be*.

Bringing the sides together

At the close of the round-robin it should be possible to see whether there is a consensus, a direction, or possibly a difference of opinion between groups. If the latter, the auditor should avoid having the groups consolidate and identify themselves *as* groups. In other words, it is good if people say 'I agree with George', but not good if they say 'George and I know because we both meet the clients. The rest of you are all wrong because . . .' Such potential conflicts must be turned away from the individual and personal, towards the actual problem and the creation of mutual understanding. As moderator, the auditor should deflect the conversation away from miniscule history or internal warfare, and get as objective a statement as possible. The auditor should ask for the alternate view immediately, giving it equal time, and again avoiding either view becoming the 'property' of a special group.

This can be done by physically facing the group with the blackboard on which the recorder summarizes the two points of view. The auditor should insist on a statement that is an accommodation of both views, rather than a win/lose argument. Ask questions such as, 'What can we say that would be agreed to by both camps?' or 'How can we phrase our understanding of the mission statement so that someone outside this room who came from either camp could support it?'

Once a core, single-sentence mission statement is reasonably firmly established (holdouts should be reminded that this is a draft, and open for renegotiation), then ask how the mission statement can be commu-nicated effectively to everyone in the organization so that they can turn it into action. Again, the auditor should use the round-robin technique to ensure that everyone has his or her say. This time, it is not necessary to look for consensus, but rather record the suggestions, problems and ingenious solutions. The round-robin should be turned into a brainstorming session. It is important to ensure that everyone has at least one turn.

Bringing the meeting to a close

If the auditor can get the focus group to accomplish all this in about three hours, he or she will have done well. With a few sentences in which people are prepared to believe, plus a great deal of information about the organization that emerged in passing, plus at least one solution, suggestion or initiative that can be incorporated into the final report (though at this moment the auditor will not know which of several that is), a great deal has been achieved.

Before saying goodbye, the auditor should again remind people that they are 'safe' – that is, the auditor will not 'inform' on them. This will create the thought that nobody in the room should inform either, and yet it does not say 'don't talk about the experience.' The auditor hopes that the focus group members will be opinion leaders who will talk in positive terms. If there are solutions, opportunities, insights and enthusiasms generated by the focus group, the auditor wants them to infect the organization with a sense of potential and accomplishment.

When the five to seven people have left, the auditor and any associates should immediately debrief themselves. The auditor should share impressions, make notes, compare notes, discuss difficulties and make lists of required information to which the focus group has drawn attention. Frequently, the auditor will find that there are questions which could be added to a questionnaire. If the questionnaire has already gone out these extra ideas can be picked up in interviews.

SUMMARY: THE FOCUS GROUP EXPERIENCE

The focus group experience offers:

- a draft mission statement;
- an overall increase in information;
- a list of unanswered questions;
- an understanding of some issues and personalities;
- a feeling for the organizational culture from the questionnaire.

These accomplishments should give the auditor a clearer sense of the direction in which the rest of the audit should go.

■ THE CASE STUDY CONTINUES

Jan. 13 Prepare focus group

Negotiating with and through Shelley for the people to be in the focus group, and getting King's approval.

Final roster

Mark Sangster, VP. (I haven't met him yet.) Used to be Manager of Accounting. Now he does something mysterious with finances. Travels a lot, sometimes taking Lisa Fremden with him.

Lisa Fremden, Manager, Design.

Daniel Scanlon, Marketing, veteran of eight years.

Carol Manning, Receptionist. (I had to battle Shelley to get her! 'Why Carol? She's just a receptionist!')

Paul Frost, Sales. (Used to be Regional Rep. for Europe.)

Ernie Stokes, Supervisor.

Bill Phipps, Machinist.

I would have liked Mariella Comeau from Transportation, but I was up to seven and there were good arguments for them all. (Why do they call it 'Transportation'? It's actually a shipping/forwarding/brokerage operation, dealing with customs, duties, manifests and all the forms necessary for sending or getting odd things to and from strange places.)

I wanted Joe Bailey as ballast. Scanlon is going to be a problem, I can feel it. Oh well, handle it now rather than later.

Jan. 15 Focus group day

And what a day it was! Ted Baxter was invaluable. Even though it's the first time I've had him work with me on an audit, he was the perfect recorder: took good notes with just the right rephrasing of extreme outbursts into useful, discussable, short statements.

I hope they all went away fairly calm and hopeful – I think they did. But half way through the day, I was afraid I'd opened a real can of worms.

Ted and I will have to go over it all again and again, but we did find out some really useful stuff.

The existing mission statement is gobbledegook, taken from a prospectus for a new product, the contract for which they never got. It talks about 'state of the art this' and 'progressive that' and is worse than useless because it could have been written by someone who had never seen the firm.

When we got around to writing a new one, there were two camps: 'We manufacture precision tools,' and 'We make custom designed instruments.' They're both right. The tools are the mainstay – '73 per cent of last year's business, and all of the profit.' (Sangster). The instruments are the up-coming thing – 'Replacing 15 per cent of traditional business each year, and more so in the future as our customers get rid of their old machines and buy new, electronically controlled gear.' (Scanlon).

The trouble is, there's an old guard who don't understand the changing circumstances. Fortunately, it's not just a generation gap. Sangster is in his sixties, but knows the score from being in the financial world and keeping up with his reading. Good old Ernie Stokes will never understand, even though he's in charge of a group of women who put together electronic equipment. (A mistake? Shelley tells me that his knowledge of metalworking is legendary in the company: he ran a lathe for 45 years.) Phipps is a belligerent young enthusiast for anything with a computer connected to it. I have my doubts about Frost, who kept on telling us about how his regular customers weren't interested in 'lights and dials and all that electronic metric nonsense with the black boxes.'

Carol Manning amazed me. Without any rhetoric, she put her finger on the other problem: highly-skilled women. It's not a case of degrees, either. The women who assemble circuits for Ernie Stokes are artists at what they do: 'the hands of brain surgeons, every one of them'. Carol pointed this out, along with the fact that they work together in isolation from the rest of the plant. (I wonder how she knows – must check this out.)

Lisa Fremden thinks she's one of the men, or as she put it 'Good design engineering is not determined by the sexual reproductive equipment of the designer.' She forgets that for all her crackerjack design abilities, she's resented by most of the managers because she only talks to her fellow designers, one or two people on the shop floor, and King. There's clearly a perception of 'us' and 'them' that is made worse by the fact that Lisa is totally unaware of it.

Ethel Walters (CEO's secretary) kept on being mentioned as a member of the 'female mafia' (Scanlon). Carol Manning defended her, but everyone else sees her as a problem – significantly excepting Lisa Fremden. Ethel guards King from people who used to have easy access to him a few years ago, but lets Lisa through any time. (Lisa denied this, but nobody was convinced.)

'Regal is a company in the process of transition into a new era for the industry,' (Scanlon). That's useful to know!

Other intuitions, confirmed by Ted:

— Design talks to (some of) Production
— Sales isn't getting the information it needs from Production, and neither of them exchange information with Marketing and Design! I couldn't believe my ears, but Ted assures me that it is so.
— Sales and Marketing and Design should be in close contact, but Fremden doesn't know how to use Market information – considers it all cosmetic, 'What do they know?' She's too wrapped up in her designs, and Marketing (Scanlon, who is very much out of step with Fremden) can't get through to her.
— Transportation. No problem. Everyone agrees it does its job.
— Accounting, ditto, remembering, of course, that according to the TRO questionnaire everyone dislikes accounting.

Fremden and Scanlon were in conversation as they left – amazing! Ted says it was engineered by Sangster. He (Sangster) shook my hand and said the afternoon had been 'interesting.' Perhaps he was aware that the TRO session generated a marked bias away from the Relationship side in just about every participant. (There was also a strong authoritarian streak – a 'right way of doing things'.) They agreed about task, and they accepted the necessity for organization, but they all saw themselves as more concerned with relationships than Regal as a whole. Will the surveys corroborate?

Chapter 6
SURVEYS

■ BENEFITS AND LIMITATIONS

Pen-and-paper surveys or questionnaires are the mainstay of communication audits because they are:

- relatively inexpensive;
- less time-consuming than interviews;
- anonymous;
- universal and standardized;
- computer-processable;
- a convenient method of obtaining overall coverage of the organization;
- easy to duplicate.

Surveys cost less in time and effort than any other methodology. However, especially in smaller organizations, anonymity is difficult to protect – at least in the eyes of the people who are filling out the survey forms. This is not so much a matter of *actual* anonymity, but of the individual respondents' *perception of* anonymity which has the effect of neutralizing answers. Nor is this paranoid fantasy: it *is* possible for extreme opinions to be identifiable, especially within a smaller organization.

Notwithstanding these problems, a universally applied questionnaire has benefits over and above the actual information received. Specifically, surveys offer:

- a (limited) opportunity for feedback, thereby generating improved morale through 'The Hawthorne Effect', whereby employees who are asked for their opinions feel better, no matter what is or is not done;
- a reminder that there is an audit in progress;
- opportunity for everyone to contribute;
- relief from objections that not everyone was consulted.

In addition to these somewhat negative and cosmetic reasons, questionnaires are particularly appropriate for the following purposes. They:

● gather demographic data (age, education, gender, length of time in position/company/profession);

● gather factual information about interests, skills and qualifications which may be out of date or 'buried' in personnel files;

● collect factual information about information flow (who talks to whom about what) that can be used in network analysis. (Note, however, that unless subjects are keeping a diary of their daily interactions, there is a tendency for a questionnaire to be answered with 'right', 'formal' or 'expected' answers);

● elicit 'write-in' comments for further investigation by interviews, focus groups, etc.;

● provide the data on which systemic (rather than personality-based) analysis and recommendations can be made.

■ DRAWING UP A SURVEY

As with all aspects of a communication audit, the object of surveys is to gain information for management decision-making. All too easily, surveys can degenerate into satisfaction evaluations, which, because they are based exclusively on feelings, are of questionable value. It is necessary to look beyond 'satisfaction' both when creating and analyzing surveys.

Whether choosing an existing survey instrument, modifying one to specific needs, or designing one from scratch, the auditor must start by asking, 'What do we need to know?' The answer should be expressed in terms of decision-making information. It might be interesting to know the ethnic origins of employees, but such a question would probably lower the credibility of the entire survey by implying possible racism, and in some jurisdictions it would also be illegal. Wanting to know about possible language problems may be a reason for asking this question legitimately, but it could generate hostility and distrust. The object of the survey is to discover patterns of interaction that can be improved by interventions that are not focused on individuals' personalities, but on objective 'work-world' behaviours that fall legitimately within the organization's framework. For example, it might solve the language issue to ask, 'Rank in order the languages you prefer to use on the job'. This is less likely to provoke the suspicion that the survey is merely 'nosing around'.

Five principles

Whether the final survey is made up in whole or in part for the specific audit, there are five principles which must be followed:

1. Clarity
2. Approval
3. Universality
4. Confidentiality
5. Lucidity

1. Clarity

The survey must be clear. Questions should be pre-tested to ensure that they are not ambiguous to the particular organization under study. (That the survey was acceptable at another time and place is no guarantee that it will be clear to this particular group of people.)

2. Approval

The survey must be officially sanctioned and formally 'backed by the CEO'. In order to have a good return sample, as many as possible of the entire organization must respond. If they do not take the exercise seriously, then they will either not hand in forms, or treat them lightly. A covering letter from the CEO encouraging participation is necessary, restating once again the anonymity of the process, emphasizing that this is not a risk-taking event, and reminding people that the audit is not designed as a punitive expedition in search of people to dismiss.

3. Universality

Everyone must have an equal opportunity to fill out the questionnaire. This means that it must be delivered and retrieved so that nobody is left out or given too little or too much time to answer.

4. Confidentiality

The survey must be processed and evaluated responsibly and objectively. This means that there should be no way that information can be traced back to its source either through direct naming or through indirect assessment. In some cases this means that information should *not* be reported in detailed statistical breakdowns, lest the readers are able to identify individuals. However, the auditor should distinguish between the final, formal and 'public' account of the results, and what he or she can glean from the survey which is too personal to be identified, but nonetheless is valid. Like the initial walk-around intuitions, these insights from the questionnaire or survey require further objectification and testing. (This is one of the most important reasons for having several instruments and comparing them.)

5. Lucidity

The process of surveying should be lucid. That is, the respondents should know that:

- the survey response sheets will be destroyed;
- the auditor and assistants are competent to manage the process and make the necessary statistical and/or mathematical operations.

If their fears are dismissed by an open statement of what the survey will accomplish, and how it will benefit each individual as well as the company, people are more likely to answer honestly and completely.

■ PRE-TESTED SURVEYS

A pre-tested survey helps to avoid many problems, but it does not eliminate them. Indeed, the misuse of questions from a published survey can lead to a failure of credibility for the auditor, especially if the wording:

- is inappropriate to the firm under study;
- is bewildering to the respondents;
- contains language not in local use.

An astute auditor discovers whether this is indeed the case by pre-testing, and then if necessary rewriting (and subsequently retesting) the questionnaire.

The auditor should always prefer the simple and direct to the generic and official-sounding: 'Do you make use of the recreational/leisure facilities?' is better expressed: 'Do you use the coffee-room on the fourth floor?' if that indeed is what you want to know.

All too often if the auditor states that he or she is conducting a survey, the management will want to ask some questions of their own. Such questions can sometimes be offensively obtrusive, redundant, vague, and even counter-productive. The auditor should be prepared to take a firm stance against such co-opting of the audit process, while still listening to management's declared needs. Often, the auditor can point out how the information that management feels it needs can be deduced from existing questions.

■ 'RIGHT ANSWERS' AND LYING

If the auditor decides to add questions of his or her own to an existing survey instrument or to design one from scratch, questions which imply a 'right answer' should be avoided. For example, the question 'Do you wish more information about . . .?' has an obvious 'right answer' of 'yes', (or 1-2 on a Likert scale), whether or not the person has any use for the information. Natural human curiosity, plus the fact of being asked, together generate a stock response. (Of course, there will be 'rogue' answers of 'No' (5 on a Likert scale), but these are also predictable in that there are always a few people who like to be individualistic.)

As well as the 'right answer syndrome', there is also the question of outright lying. Pardonable exaggeration or wishful thinking are not the same thing as the deliberate fabrication of answers that have no relationship to reality; and yet occasionally personnel are so dissatisfied with an organization that this can happen. This shouldn't come as a surprise to the auditor, because an unhealthy communication environment would in all probability manifest itself in management problems including (but not limited to) absenteeism, high turnover, general dissatisfaction and low morale.

The best way in which to generate honest responses in any organization is to ensure that the five basic rules (outlined above) are followed scrupulously. Making up long questionnaires which 'lie detect' by approaching the same subject by different verbal routes is not appropriate for a small organization because it is simpler to ask people directly in an interview where relevant context directs the answer. In addition, the response to long questionnaires is predictably poorer than to shorter formats.

■ PHYSICAL DESIGN OF SURVEYS

The format and layout of a survey questionnaire is important to its success. The auditor should note the following.

(a) Take time to type, word process or print the questions in such a way that they are:

- easy to read;
- easy to answer (room for checks, circles, comments);
- easy to score.

It is important that no one of these three prejudices the other two. Avoid inscrutable scoring, or boxes or numbers which may baffle the respondents.

(b) Provide the respondents with a simple guide to the questionnaire form. Start out by telling them (again) why they are being surveyed, what kind of information will result, and what it will be used for. Remind them that their anonymity will be protected. Tell them approximately how long it will take them to answer the questions. Explain how to record the answers, and provide examples of how to do it correctly. Give clear instructions about what to do with the questionnaire when it is completed.

(c) Consider the forms of answers which should be invited. Survey instruments can invite answers in many forms. From the more to the less constraining, they are:

- yes/no (or forced choice);
- Likert scale numbered (1 2 3 4 5);
- Likert scale words (agree strongly, agree, neutral, disagree, disagree strongly);
- rank order of preferences;
- choose one (or more) from a list;
- write-in (or open ended).

Each has advantages and disadvantages. Forced-choice questions are best for discovering facts, scaled questions for opinions, open ended for suggestions. The auditor's confidence in the representativeness of answers is strongest when most of the respondents agree, whether this is by making the same written-in suggestion or by circling the same number on a scale of preferences.

(d) Consider the type of questions to be asked. Questions should be:

- mutually exclusive;
- exhaustive;
- categorized by a single principle.

The auditor should avoid overlapping questions or questions that ask the same thing in different ways, since both contribute to confusion in the mind of the respondent. Similarly, it is important to ensure that there is not some other category to a question which has not been mentioned, for example, a missing age classification or an 'other' that the respondents have not been allowed to choose. A single principle of organizing and categorizing avoids questions that ask the respondent to choose among different *kinds* of alternatives that belong in different questions. (An example of this mistake is the confusion of communication *sources* and communication *channels* by asking for a choice among: a) telephone, b) written memo, c) face-to-face instructions, d) orders from immediate supervisor.)

The auditor should be consistent in the format of questions. Respondents should not be asked to tick one question, and then to circle another.

There is a sample questionnaire on page 167. Note how it inquires into:

- how people *get* information;
- how they *give* it;
- by what *channels* they give and get it;
- how they *prefer* to give and get it;
- some measures of *quality* of information (timeliness, style);
- some indications of the information *content*;
- some assessment of job *satisfaction*;
- *demographic* data.

Particular attention should be paid to the demographic information to ensure that it is not ridiculous (asking how many people have worked for 20 years in a 10 year old organization), or overly detailed (asking for specific degrees when only a very few people possess them).

The questionnaire should be introduced by a letter from the CEO as illustrated in Fig. 6.1.

President's Office
Regal Instruments

To all staff

This questionnaire is part of the communication audit being conducted on Regal by Pat Smith. Please take the time to fill it in today.
Completed forms should be sealed in the enclosed envelope, and placed in the collecting boxes beside the elevators on each floor.

None of the information collected on these forms will be identified with you, and the forms will be destroyed when the information has been encoded for statistical analysis.

If you have any questions, please call Pat Smith on extension xxxx.

I am convinced that the information gathered through this entire communication audit will prove to be of benefit to Regal Instruments, and all those who work in it.

Sincerely,

J. B. King
President, Regal Instruments

Figure 6.1 A sample letter introducing a questionnaire

■ TURNING COMPLETED QUESTIONNAIRES INTO DATA

The use of computers

For many years, statisticians generally considered that a population of up to 200 (statistically speaking, N or the total number of people = 200) can be handled without recourse to a computer. Today, however, there are programs that can be mounted on a personal computer that are as powerful as those which used to require mainframes. Although it is possible to analyze small populations with pencil and paper methods, a computer's flexibility, speed of computation, reliability and freedom from mechanical errors makes its use virtually mandatory.

Between the stack of completed questionnaire forms and the computer stands the code sheet. This is a page of squared paper which digests all the answers into numbers that can be programmed into a computer. Typically, each question will have at least one more 'box' than there are possible responses. For example, if you ask a question on the Likert scale of 5, your compilation sheet will have a box for each of the possible responses, plus one for 'no response'.

Every yes/no question you asked will generate at least three possible responses (yes, no, no answer), times the total number of respondents. A Likert-scale question will generate at least six possible responses, times the number of respondents.

In other words, the audit involves more numbers than a person can hold in his or her head and convert into data, and then manipulate and interpret into information. In short, we need a computer.

Since each brand of computer and program is individual, it is not appropriate to spell out in detail exactly how to load numbers into the machine that is available. The auditor will either already have such a machine and be familiar with such programs, or will not. In the latter case the auditor must either take courses, go through an intensive period of self-training, or subcontract the programming to a person with computer expertise. It is sometimes possible to use the organization's computing services to handle data analysis. In such a case, where a company employee is encoding and manipulating data, it is very important to preserve anonymity by keeping private all names or other identifications. The operator should see only the code sheet, never the completed questionnaires.

An appropriate program for handling a communication audit is a statistical software package of the kind available for many personal computers. There are a number of statistical, accounting and general purpose programs that can be used. The basic operations which the auditor needs to be able to do are:

● tabulation and cross-tabulation;

- mode, mean and median calculations;
- percentages;
- assessment of statistical validity.

It is very useful and time-efficient if the computer program will also generate graphs and charts that can be inserted into the text of the report, or can be turned into overhead transparencies for the final presentation.

Applying basic statistical techniques

Although the auditor does not need to be a statistician, an understanding of some basic statistical concepts is essential. The most important of these is that the science of statistics enables us to compare the results we have observed in the real world to what would happen if the numbers were generated by 'blind chance'. Statistics will tell us whether and to what degree the numbers we have collected are 'significant', that is, the likelihood that they are *not* the result of chance. Computer programs exist that contain the necessary formulae for calculating these odds, into which it is only necessary for the programmer to insert the data, and then allow the program to make the necessary mathematical manipulations.

The manipulations are of two kinds: tendencies and significance.

Tendencies

There are three basic ways in which to look at the results of data collected – as in the most effective questionnaires – on a Likert scale: the mean (average), the median (midpoint), and the mode (most frequent value). Each has appropriate uses.

The mean is the 'balance point' of a range of numbers. It invites the next question, 'Is it normally distributed, or is it positively or negatively biased?'. For example, in the question asked about age, the output from the computer program might show that the average age of a group of 30 people is 38. One might be tempted to generalize prematurely about this organization if one did not go on to ask the computer to show how the ages were distributed as in Fig. 6.2.

Even mere inspection of this graph suggests that quite a few of the assumptions implied by the phrase 'average age 38' are misleading. For one thing, the results are not 'normally distributed', that is, they are not tidily shaped in a smooth curve with the largest number of instances in the middle column. If we ask 'What is the median or midpoint?' of these columns, we would find that it is 45, which is the age at which there is the same number of people both older and

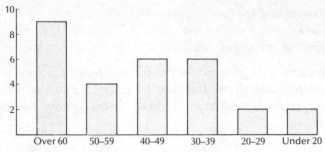

Figure 6.2 Distribution of ages within an organization

younger. Clearly, however, it is the modal category in which we find the greatest number of instances (column 1) that interests us most, and to a lesser extent, columns 3 and 4.

Significance
The significance of statistics can be measured by mathematical tests. Simply, these tests compare the actual results with those which might be obtained through random chance. If the results of the survey are random, they are non-significant in statistical terms – the same results could have been generated by monkeys banging indiscriminately on typewriters, and are hence without meaning. Significance is measured between 0 (no element of chance), and 1 (completely random). A value of 0.05 or less is usually accepted as good evidence of significance for samples of 500 or less.

Most of the time, a communication audit will survey everyone in the organization. Thus the questions about sampling error which are so important to mass communication studies do not arise.

Once the auditor has inserted results into a computer program, initially the computer should generate the basic frequencies of the different responses. The basic frequencies are the number of times that each possible answer was chosen, set out by the individual questions. The mean, mode and median scores from each question should be plotted and inspected for significance (that is, the auditor should look at the numbers to see if they seem interesting). From this first assessment, the auditor will probably want to make observations such as, 'Average (mean) scores are 2 on the Likert scale, indicating that in general, people are pleased with the information they receive', or 'The score appearing most often (mode) in answering the question concerning feedback was 4 on the Likert scale, indicating that most people are not happy with this aspect of communication'.

Before making such statements, the auditor should check the significance evaluation done by the computer program to be sure that numbers are not being assessed when they are actually non-significant, that is, could have occurred by chance.

There is much more that can be done, the most important of which is cross-tabulation.

Cross-tabulation

Cross-tabulation is simply the pouring together of data from two or more different sets of answers. For example, if one question asks 'How much information do you want?' the answers may look like this:

Scale (a great deal) 1	2	3	4	5 (a little)
%	3	27	40	26	4

Not much can be concluded from this table except perhaps that most people are reasonably content with the information flow. If, however, the auditor cross-tabulates with the question about gender, a more informative set of results is created. The auditor should check the probability calculation on most programs as a value for p, where any value *less than* 0.05 indicates that the relationship between the two elements of the cross-tabulation is significant as opposed to accidental. The same question can be asked:

Scale (a great deal) 1		2		3		4		5 (a little)	
Gender	M	F	M	F	M	F	M	F	M	F
%	1	2	10	17	27	13	22	4	0	4

From these cross-tabulated results, we can see that the women want more information than the men. If the program used generates percentages as well as raw scores, this becomes very clear. (The above example is based on N = 100 for simplicity.)

Cross-tabulation allows the auditor to discover sub-groups within the larger population, and to understand these groups better. For example, those who have been with the company longer are more satisfied than those who have joined recently. This is information useful to decision making since it allows the problem to be addressed directly, for example by meetings, letters or other opportunities to communicate with the target group – without necessarily involving the other group(s) who might be bored or resentful.

Cross-tabulation is useful when immediate results seem to be bland and insignificant, since small sub-groups can 'hide' or 'cancel each other out' in a large population.

Most usually, one aspect of cross-tabulation will be a demographic question (age, gender, length of time with the company, education, etc.) and the other an opinion-based question in which the auditor suspects that the average (mean) conceals pockets of significant information. These are groups of people who have expressed the same opinions on the same question. It is not necessary to cross-tabulate all questions against each other (and it is quite expensive in time and paper to do so); however, the auditor should use the demographic information to analyze most opinion or preference questions.

In auditing a small organization it is not always necessary to use a heroic scale of computerized analysis to interpret such responses. Further questioning in focus groups or interviews will often be more accurate and specific about wants and needs when the auditor knows from the survey where the significant areas are. Obviously, the auditor must be both tactful and responsible about sensitive issues. No one should be singled out as a complainer, nor should the minority group as a whole be put at risk – or at what they perceive to be risk.

Problematic results

From time to time, a graph of a set of results shows that there are two concentrations of opinion, some positive and some negative. On a Likert scale of one to five questions, the results look like those in Fig. 6.3.

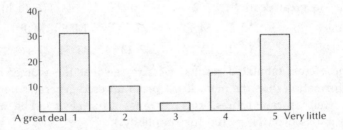

Figure 6.3 A graph illustrating answers to a Likert scale question

This response, which is called 'bimodal' because it has two modes, tells us that there is disagreement, but not about what. It could be that there is deeply entrenched hostility within the organization, in which case, we need to be able to recognize the groups. Cross-tabulations of age, gender, or length of service might resolve the problem, or at least enable us to ask appropriate people.

Alternatively, the problem may be confusion in the way the question has been interpreted – in other words, it may be a pseudo-problem which the auditors have generated. It is useful to return to the actual questionnaires and decide whether there are real differences of opinion, or whether quite simply a number of people misunderstood the wording of the question. The auditor should remember that an error of this kind if it is discovered, can be perfectly acceptable as the consequence of dealing with the real world. However, the auditor could live to regret the error of interpreting that a difference of opinion existed where there in fact was none. If this mistake is discovered by the organization at the stage of the final report, it could undermine the credibility of the whole study.

■ THE CASE STUDY CONTINUES

Jan. 15 Survey approval
A whole day's work on getting the survey approved. One very late night's work brought me back to schedule. Shelley proved to be meticulous – caught me on the point of leaving no space for technical qualifications, as if all education were at a university!

J. B. King, luckily I caught him before he went off for the next five days, had endless questions about the form, the format, the questions themselves, and, predictably, wanted to ask a few of his own. I persuaded him that his question about the building would be better handled in interviews, largely because I couldn't get him away from the most biased formulations that invited only approval.

These late nights have to end soon! However, letting myself out of the building, I met Patrick Shaughnessey, head of maintenance. He's about 25, plump and inconspicuous, but an entrepreneur. I wonder if J. B. King knows he's using the job as a means of building up an office-cleaning business. Patrick has a squad of women at his command who mop, dust, vacuum, water plants – the whole range of maintenance, and all in the dead of night. He's electrician, plumber, the lot. He was certainly ready for anything: I met him pushing a little cart with every conceivable tool strapped to it. My tape-recorder was no problem to him, so I interviewed him on the spot, trusting that I remembered the interview protocols. Interesting stuff. This one gets transcribed by me: I wouldn't want it in the hands of someone inside Regal. He concluded by saying, 'I'll be out of here in three weeks, but I'll be back for certain. You just forget about Maintenance in your report. I'll see to that.' (I played the tape back twice, and that's exactly what he said.) Is it a riddle?

Jan. 21
Spent most of the day getting the surveys picked up. Thanks to Shelley, everyone was forewarned except Sales, which had forgotten to set aside time. Except for predictable absences that I'll try to catch in the next couple of days, I've got a fairly good coverage now – 88 per cent – with the chance of getting nearly everyone by the end of the week.

Jan. 22 First survey results
Preliminary statistical results are in. I've got corroboration of the gaps between Marketing and Design and the isolation of Sales, but not very

strongly. I think that there are too many people telling me what I want to hear, or what J. B. King wants to hear. Still, I've got some trends that if not impressive mathematically, are nonetheless significant.

There's an interesting clique of women in Production that needs corroboration by the network analysis. I doubt if I'd have seen it if I hadn't been entering the results onto the sheets.

I cross-tabulated the bland answers to the benefits package questions against age and gender. It falls out that the women, especially the younger ones, are not happy, but their unhappiness was buried in the totals. I'm willing to bet there's no maternity leave here.

The anomaly is that nobody's getting information from the top, save in the form of orders, they're all wanting to know what's happening next, and yet they trust senior management. This doesn't seem reasonable. I must be missing something, but I still have several interviews to go, thanks to some poor scheduling today.

Chapter 7
NETWORK ANALYSIS

Network analysis in a practical organizational context is the making of maps that connect time, space and communication. It is based on counting communication interactions between people, that is, every conversation, telephone call, letter or meeting of each person in the organization. Since this would be an impossible task without limitations, network analysis is usually done in 'snapshots' or short, intensive periods of time when people can be relied upon to record all (or most) interactions. The resulting 'communication maps' can assist in the identification of opportunities and problems, such as communication nodes and bottlenecks. Network analysis can guide the auditor towards suggesting useful changes to formal communication, and can lead to the restructuring of both formal and informal channels so that they complement each other.

Network analysis is concerned with flow rather than content, and finds out who is talking to whom, and to a lesser extent, through what channels. Finding out what is being said comes from further exploration through interviews, surveys and focus groups. Network analysis can nevertheless assist the analysis of content of communication by helping the auditor to understand the web of interactions that otherwise would take months within the organization to discover (and even then not fully comprehend). Network analysis has as its focus interactions between people, where what is at issue is *total* communication – including emotions, attitudes and beliefs. It is based on the 'convergence theory', whereby communication is the deciding factor in the creation of new mutually-held attitudes which are the source of active decision making. Simply stated, if people interact a lot, they are more likely to share opinions, goals and aims than if they merely send each other occasional orders.

In the audit process network analysis is mostly used in conjunction with other, corroborating instruments. It helps the auditor by:

● identifying potential members for a focus group;
● suggesting material to investigate (sometimes to correct or show misperceptions) in interviews;

● assisting evaluation of surveys — particularly when 'information needs' are assessed in order to discover whether they are 'real' or merely the results of curiosity.

Network analysis is particularly useful as it helps the auditor understand the context in which each person interviewed works, since a person's contacts and environment are a controlling factor in his or her communication.

A network analysis may be elaborated by asking people to note the reason for each interaction. In an open, vibrant organization, this can lead to a valuable understanding of the informal web of communication that goes beyond passing on official orders. However, in a closed, unresponsive organization such a request can lead to lying or self-justification in the fear of being disciplined for indulging in 'unproductive chit-chat'. It is particularly useful – and much less threatening – to know whether a person is responding to or initiating calls, as this can lead to important discoveries about upward, downward and lateral information flows.

■ WAYS OF CONDUCTING A NETWORK ANALYSIS

Network analysis can also be done mechanically (by examining computerized lists of long-distance telephone calls), or non-intrusively by observation (by standing in the corner with a clipboard and hand-counting device). However, nobody is invisible; in other words, intrusiveness is a matter of degree.

Another, not so productive method is 'snowball sampling', that is, picking several individuals at random, discovering their primary contacts, then finding the people with whom the contacts interact, and so on. Essentially, this is a description of what an intuitive auditor does without knowing it, and a more sophisticated auditor controls with surveys and other instruments. Snowball, or 'small world' sampling, where the auditor is looking for the snowballs of interlinked people to coalesce, is not very reliable, although it can be useful in showing the larger context of communication and breaking the perception that the organization exists apart from the rest of the world.

Network analysis for practical research (as opposed to academic study) has limits to its effectiveness as a stand-alone methodology, but it enhances all other methodologies because it is *not* content-specific and thus gives a sense of total information flow. On the basis of a network analysis, physical location can be altered, group membership modified, isolated members of staff reabsorbed into the network, and bottlenecks identified and expanded.

The auditor can perform a network analysis with the compliance of those studied or less intrusively by observation. In either event, what the auditor is striving for is a *complete* record over a given time (which can be quite short if repeated or checked) of who talks to whom. *All* connections. *All* instances. Completeness is vital – including all contacts, whether job-related or not. This can be difficult, because non-job or *apparently* non-job communication is frowned upon in many organizations. This is why merely asking people 'Who do you talk with in a normal day?' will not do. One specific, average day must be chosen and the test must be run in such a way as to catch everyone. Because of absences, etc., it is often necessary to hold more than one such 'N-Day'.

■ PREPARING FOR NETWORK ANALYSIS

The auditor should follow these steps.

(a) Give each person a form and a list of all the people in the organization, and ask them to check off *each* interaction on the form with a tick or cross and the time any interaction takes place during the day. Have extra lines for writing in external contacts either individually by name, or generically (supplier, customer, enquiry, complaint, etc.).

(b) Make instructions clear and simple. Pre-test forms and instructions with a small random group. Arrange to deliver the forms so that everyone is ready to start at the same time. A good method (if the numbers are not too formidable) is to hand deliver the forms, instruction sheets and return envelopes to each person the day before. This way problems of interpretation can be solved one-to-one, ahead of time.

(c) Give people, such as receptionists who interact with a great number of people in any given day, special help in setting up their forms so that they can handle them efficiently. Writing in each name is not appropriate, but with the help of the person involved, it is possible to set up a form that will record the interactions with check-marks, and incidentally simplify the eventual transcription of the data.

The format in Fig. 7.1 will be adequate for most people in any organization, although some may find it too detailed and revealing. Be flexible, and do not stimulate unnecessary reactions by asking for what some people will regard as private information. Similarly, it may not always be reasonable to ask for exact times – 'am' or 'pm', plus the sequence of the notation may be all that people are willing and able to provide.

NETWORK ANALYSIS FORM

For this one day only, (*insert date and day*), use this form to keep a record of *all* your interactions with people both inside and outside the company. Write in the names of the people you deal with – be sure to include surnames! Check the attached list of people in the organization if you need to do so.

If you *initiate* the conversation, visit or telephone call, underline your entry.

If you are the person who *responds* to the conversation, visit or telephone call, just note the name and time.

If you visit or have a visitor for a face-to-face meeting, write *V* beside the time.

If you telephone or are telephoned, write *P*.

If you get or send a written communication (letter, memo, etc.) write *W*.

If you interact with someone who is not a part of the organization, note this down as *customer* or *supplier* or simply as *outside contact*, if you cannot easily identify the relationship to you and the organization.

If you meet with several people in a formal or informal meeting (such as over your lunchtime, or in a formal meeting), list their names in a separate group, with the time, at the bottom of the page.

For example:

Name	Type and time of communication
Bill Murphy	*P* 9:15 *P* 10:35 *V* 2:05 *P* 2:30 *V* 3:20
Carol Fredericks	*V* 11:15
Jim MacDonald	*P* 9:20
Customer A	*P* 9:35 *P* 11:25 *P* 2:20
Customer B	*V* 3:45
FPY Co. (supplier)	*W* 4:10

Meetings
Bill, Jim, Harry Foster, Gail Markham + two guests – lunch, 12:00.
Bill, Jim – meeting with customer, 3:45.

Finally, before handing in this form, please answer the following question:

How would you describe today's work-load? (Circle the appropriate number)

1	2	3	4	5
Below routine		Typical of routine		Above routine

Figure 7.1 A detailed network analysis form

Network analysis can be counter-productive and its results distorted if over detailed. More than most instruments, it must be tailored to the nature of the particular organization. No matter how simple it is, however, it can provide a great deal of information which is referred to during the course of the audit.

■ STUDYING THE DATA

When all the forms are received, the auditor will have a great deal of information that can be used in a variety of ways, provided it is re-organized to make it accessible and meaningful. The first task is to discover the frequency, flow and appropriateness of the communications that the forms represent. This can be dealt with by either a 'macro' or a 'micro' approach.

The macro approach

The macro approach is to create a simplified master chart that records the total number (and possibly the type) of interactions that each person enters into. This identifies the frequent communicators, isolated members of staff and those who carry an average communication load. It also identifies groups of people who set a norm for their type of work.

This information can be revealing when tested by the criterion of appropriateness. For instance, it may be discovered that three section heads receive and send approximately the same number of communications, thereby establishing a norm. The fourth section may both send and receive almost twice as many as the norm, and the fifth a third less than the norm. When the interaction frequencies for their respective secretaries or receptionists are checked, it is possible that the communication frequency for the secretaries varies inversely with their bosses. The next step is to find out whether the bosses who have high and low communication frequencies are being inappropriately screened by their 'gatekeeper' secretaries. In this way, the network study will direct the auditor to a line of enquiry that can be followed up through interviews to provide useful information on the basis of which recommendations can be made that will improve the communication flows of at least four people – the secretaries who do not follow the norm for their type of work and their bosses.

The auditor can also discover the high-frequency communicators from the simplified master chart, and then find out whether they are communicating appropriately. For instance, ask whether it is reasonable that some secretaries appear to be much more active than receptionists who theoretically should be redirecting calls past the secretaries. In this way it may be discovered (and later explained in the report) that incoming calls go through two or three people before reaching their destination, or that some secretaries are functioning inappropriately as receptionists. (The reason for this may be entirely contingent upon the way in which the organization's telephone numbers are listed in the directory, or it could be that inappropriate or inadequate instructions have been given to both secretaries and receptionists as to what they can answer themselves and what they must refer to some person in authority.)

The micro approach

The micro approach is to group the forms together by department, section and group of people whose forms indicate that they communicate regularly. As shown in Fig. 7.2, chart in a matrix how the people within these units interact.

Transportation

	1	2	3	4	5	6	7	8	9	10	11	12
1	X				v		p					
2		X			v				v			
3			X		v				v			
4				X	v							
5	v		v	v	X	v		w		v	p	p
6					v	X				v		
7					p		X					
8					p			X				
9			v		p				X			
10		v			p					X		
11					v	v					X	
12					w							X

Figure 7.2 A communication matrix

In the diagram, the people designated 1 to 6 are part of a section, and those represented by 7-12 are those who interact with them. Reading across shows the contacts the individuals initiated, reading down shows to whom they responded. Thus 5 initiated contacts with everyone except 2, 7 and 9, and was contacted by everyone on the matrix. (It is possible to draw up a simpler matrix that puts contacts both initiated and received in the same cell, but the initiated/responded distinction is lost.)

From this matrix, it is possible to draw a network diagram. The most frequent communicator is obviously number 5, who therefore gets placed in the middle. The others in the section cluster around, and the external contacts are 'outside' the clique. For the purpose of demonstrating that external contacts were made on different occasions, they are separated out. Finally, the diagram is labelled to make it relevant, but not to identify individuals by name.

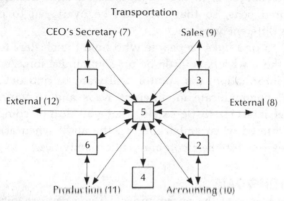

Figure 7.3 A communication network diagram

From this visual display it is possible to gain a better understanding of the way in which an organization functions – provided the diagrams do not become over-complicated. Phone calls, written and face-to-face contacts are here all subsumed into one, although it is possible to imagine other diagrams that might demonstrate these different channels, the information for which has been 'captured' in the matrix. (The convention of arrow-heads designates senders and receivers.)

Some people get asked a lot of questions, and other people do a lot of asking – or at least are initiators of contacts – but not all such people are official sources of information, such as supervisors. These frequent communicators are easily identifiable in a matrix diagram. Their interactions may well be entirely appropriate and the natural result of having the expertise of an experienced person in the section, or one who is willing to help others. Such people are particularly appropriate choices for focus groups and interviews.

Groupings (called cliques in network analysis terminology) may not be 'official' – that is, designated by the formal organizational chart. Equally, they may exactly mirror formal departments and sections. In either case, look for the liaison people who span boundaries into other cliques or formal sections. Sometimes these interactions will be official cross-group transactions, as in the case of managers who meet regularly. Sometimes they will be appropriate but not official in that they cross section boundaries without going through the formal chain of command, as in the case of two or more people who work on the same project even though they are in different sections or departments. Sometimes interactions may be inappropriate, as in the case of a person who has a 'pipeline' around his or her boss to one of the senior executives. (In practice, people rarely confess to such connections.)

A useful technique is to draw diagrams on clear acetate using different coloured pens, so that they can be overlaid to compare or contrast the different versions.

It is usual to find *links* or people who hold the clusters together and *isolates*, or those who have little or no communication. As a result of having this information, the auditor will want to find out why members of staff communicate in different ways and to varying degrees through brief interviews. (Be careful that you do not compromise the anonymity offered when embarking on the audit when asking people about the reasons for their communication activities.)

■ INTERPRETING DATA

In either the macro or the micro approach you can organize and interpret your information in a variety of ways, including:

● Conceptual
● Spatial
● Organizational
● Temporal

Conceptual

When you have constructed network diagrams of the sections and departments, there are some conclusions that can be drawn from the configurations themselves. Network research has shown that some organizational principles have strengths and weaknesses. The possibilities include:

● the chain
● the circle
● the wheel
● the Y-fork

The chain

A communication chain with the supervisor at the end is fast if the messages are simple and related to specific tasks. The chain is dependent upon the leader, and functions only if there is strong discipline.

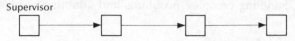

Figure 7.4 A communication chain

The wheel

A communication wheel with the supervisor in the middle is fast, task related, stable and leader dependent, but is a poor morale-builder, slow to change and not characteristic of groups solving complex problems.

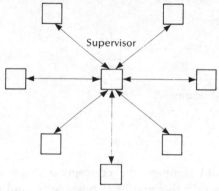

Figure 7.5 A communication wheel

The circle

A communication circle – a shared-information network – is slow, not very accurate, unstable; but adapts well to change since it is *not* leader dependent and has excellent potential for good morale. It is a characteristic configuration for the solving of complex problems.

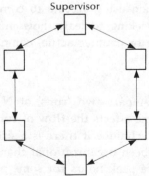

Figure 7.6 A communication circle

The Y-fork

A communication Y, where one person channels communication like a switch in a railway line, is like the chain, but has divided authority lines. It is fast, leader dependent and accurate, but it is poor for morale, for handling complex problems and adapting to change.

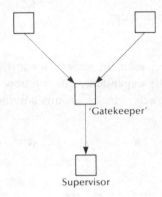

Figure 7.7 A communication Y

Spatial

The auditor should compare the conceptual maps with the physical locations of people. In this way it is possible to find out how physical location affects communication, either reinforcing or denying communication. Acetate charts of the office layout can be overlaid with the arrows drawn from the spider-web diagrams to show this clearly.

Organizational

The auditor should compare the conceptual and spatial maps with the organization chart, again using acetate to compare diagrams. At this stage, the auditor is seeking to learn how much the formal lines of responsibility reinforce or counter actual communication.

Temporal

The auditor should compare two 'runs' of N-day (network analysis day) to see whether time affects the flow of communication. (This is a particularly powerful technique if there is a sizeable time-gap between runs, or if there have been organizational changes.) Times of day can be compared. Are there peak hours for some people or groups? Why? (Interviewing will uncover the reasons.)

■ USING COMPUTERS

For most business applications involving small numbers of people (around 200), a computer is not a necessity for a useful network analysis. Sophisticated programs exist capable of drawing scattergrams, networks, and matrices, and undoubtedly some of these will soon be available on micro computers. Any program capable of arranging numbers in a matrix and converting the results into plots and diagrams, or ordering by frequency, will be of help to a network analysis. Although research purists may be offended by the flexibility of this approach, it is justifiable when one considers that the purpose is the description of an individual organization rather than the enunciation of theory. Moreover, because network analysis is not used independently, but rather triangulated with other instruments, it need not have the detailed accuracy necessary in a stand-alone methodology.

You may want to return to your network analysis data later in the audit process to corroborate or make sense of information you have discovered through other instruments. For instance, you may suspect that there is a 'secretaries' network' that is an entirely unofficial but an organizationally crucial source of information about, for instance, who is where at what time. Such networks usually carry much more than information directly relevant to functional matters: they are the transmission lines for gossip and much more importantly the myths and legends that constitute the corporate culture.

■ THE TYPICAL DAY

The final question about how typical the day was for each person should be loaded into the same program used for the statistical analysis of the survey. From this, the auditor can discover how the people felt about their day, thereby checking the assumption that N-day was indeed reasonably typical. In fact, this question is more a means of demonstrating the auditor's choice, in that after the network information is placed before people in the form of a report, there are always those who claim that the day in question was not typical for reasons which always seem persuasive to them, but which are nonetheless not statistically significant.

The auditor is not attempting to state that the information gleaned from N-day is absolute, only that it is *representative*. So long as the day in question is 80 per cent typical, it is adequate for audit purposes. The auditor is not intending to tell the organization that things 'always' or 'never' happen the way they appear in the network analysis charts, only that they are typical. The auditor wants to concentrate on something other than the non-typical events that stick in people's minds simply because they are *not* routine, and thereby make it possible to point to the fact that one person is involved in four times the communication activity of another, or that some people are isolated from each other who should be in constant if not daily contact. In other words, this is not an exact science, but it is indicative, and as such provides persuasive evidence for the overall audit.

■ THE CASE STUDY CONTINUES

Jan. 26 Network analysis

The network analysis went quite well, and I don't think it needs to be repeated. Almost everyone responded, with a few predictable exceptions who were covered indirectly by the people with whom they interacted.

Accounting and Transportation are wheels; Production a series of straight lines leading to several cliques that function on their own; Marketing with only three people is remarkable for its lack of outside links and liaisons; Sales (predictably) is a wheel focused on the secretary; and there is a classic Y formation at the top, with the CEO's secretary the bottleneck.

As far as interlinks among departments are concerned, there aren't nearly enough, and very few among the section heads. This is appropriate in the case of Accounting and Transportation, where there is a lot of communication that doesn't go (and doesn't need to go) through the head. Cliques in Production, and isolates include one VP and one manager (of course!), the elusive head of Maintenance.

Now to set this out in diagrams which don't 'point a finger', but are nonetheless useful. Perhaps this is a subject which should be taken up with King in the interim report. It's certainly not for public consumption, or everyone will be reading in far too much into it.

Carol must have a boyfriend in Production. They both reported the contact on their forms! That's why she is so well informed! There's another of those grapevine links between Sales and Production, and I think it would be possible to demonstrate a 'secretaries' network' in a clique that's headed by Ethel Walters.

Chapter 8

INTERVIEWS

Interviews are a means of finding out what people think as a result of holding the positions and doing the jobs that they do. Unlike focus groups that encourage people to think about the organization as a whole and become 'we-focused', interviews are more personal and 'I-focused'.

Interviews take time, and are not entirely quantifiable, but they are by far the most productive way of coming to grips with an organization and its component individuals. Interviews should be structured, so that nobody feels slighted, and yet also have room for open-ended comments by the interviewees.

Interviews during a communication audit:

● clarify formal and informal communication structure;
● reveal content of jobs and roles;
● help define the values of the organization's culture;
● identify the effects of individual personalities.

■ MAINTAINING OBJECTIVITY

The seductive temptation that faces the auditor is to reverse the above order of importance and concentrate on personalities. However, to do so is to lose objectivity and allow the audit to fall victim to the auditor's own likes and dislikes. This is not to say that the auditor cannot enjoy the human interaction with and the individuality of those interviewed, and it certainly does not suggest that the auditor becomes a machine that reads questions from a clip-board.

If the auditor systematically asks the same questions of all those interviewed, the differences among their answers will throw light on the formal and informal communication structure, and expose any conflict between these two modes of interaction. It is to that conflict that the auditor should address his or her attention. Resolution of interpersonal conflicts is not the auditor's job. However, concentrating on the objective, impersonal aspects of the communication structure will frequently take interviewees to a different level of awareness in which they can abandon some of their animosities as they realize that the problem is not another person's fault, but a defect that can be systematically corrected.

Interviews show what both the individuals and the company do. Unlike focus groups, that show directly in the relatively public language people use when talking in a group, the one-to-one context of an interview causes people to talk more revealingly about their pride in (or dislike of) the work they do. Since some degree of personal revelation is inescapable, interviews must be treated as confidences, and only quoted when dealing with objective fact or with the interviewee's permission.

An auditor is not a licenced psychiatrist, nor should he or she pretend to be one. The auditor should find out more about the organization's goals, objectives, products or services from the interviews. This knowledge gives focus to the eventual recommendations, because it is shared, public information that relates to organizational goals rather than to personal agendas. If the auditor can show people how this or that change in communication structure, equipment or patterns can improve the end product, he or she is doing the job. Saying that people will be happier or feel more fulfilled if they attend to each others' personal quirks and foibles is not providing either effective insight or pragmatic motivation towards change. The senior executives of an organization can legitimately require employees to use a communication system, whether it be memos, telephones or computers: they cannot order people to be nicer to each other.

■ WHOM AND WHERE TO INTERVIEW

The people who should be interviewed are:

● the leaders of the organization and its sections and sub-sections;
● representatives of those who are led.

In other words, interviewing follows the formal lines of communication within the organization, and includes more people who are at the top than are lower in the hierarchy.

Interviews work best if the interviewees go to the auditor, rather than the other way around. This approach puts the auditor in control. Specific advantages include the following.

● The auditor is on his or her own 'turf', and thus immediately has more control not only over interruptions, but also over the whole process of the interview.
● The interviewees bring only themselves. That is, they do not have recourse to memory-aids such as files and notes which can often be used to obscure an answer rather than to make it more useful.

● The interviewees are able to see the auditor in action. This should be more than just watching him or her sit at a desk and take notes: the room should reflect what is going on. Organizational charts, building plans, network surveys, focus-group reports and mission statements should all be visible in wall-size posters-in-the-making, with questions, comments and 'to do' lists on or beside them. (The auditor should beware of making these too specific, or confidentiality will be compromised.)

This paraphernalia of the auditor's trade is not only useful to the auditor, but it also is very interesting to the visitor. Interviewees should be allowed to 'nose around' and look at the charts and diagrams: they should find their places in the 'pictures' of the organization. This causes them to start the interview with a determination to make their names and functions memorable, to add to the 'pictures', as compared to grudgingly granting a few minutes in their office and at their convenience.

■ HOW TO INTERVIEW
The psychologist Carl Roger gave his name to a style of interviewing that is now called 'Rogerian'. It is characterized by being:
● non-judgemental;
● non-directive.

Roger developed this style for the psychiatric interview, but its application to a communication audit is both ethical and effective. The Rogerian interview invites the interviewee to solve his or her own problems. The interviewer's role is to ask questions that clarify (as opposed to leading, revealing, personal or embarrassing questions). The interviewer offers only comments that 'play back' what the interviewee said earlier. These are the interviewer's way of dealing with inconsistencies and contradictions – the auditor points them out, and lets the interviewee solve the problems they impose.

Questions such as, 'How do you feel about that?' or comments by the interviewer that overtly investigate emotions and feelings should be avoided. Interviewees may reveal hostility, anger, hurt, insult and a variety of other emotions, and it is acceptable that they do so. It is not ethical for a communication auditor to exploit or magnify these emotions. The auditor should acknowledge them, but neither approve nor disapprove them. Rather, the auditor should focus on what that person can do, as opposed to feel.

People often attempt to create a good impression by the 'suffering servant' ploy. That is, they tell stories about how they have been wronged, or concerning how unfairly hard they work, in the hopes that the auditor will champion them and their cause. Whether the auditor does or not (preferably not), they will frequently take the attitude expressed in the statement, 'Well, I'll try harder, I'll improve my attitude'. This is a plea to be liked, not an effective way of improving the situation. Again, the auditor should neither approve nor disapprove, because to do so would feed the interviewee's inappropriate behaviour. Rather, the discussion should be steered back to what can be done in terms of concrete action by a question that the interviewee can answer, such as, 'What changes would you recommend that would solve the problem?' If the interviewee merely cycles around to complain again about personalities, the auditor should consider cutting losses and moving on. Sometimes, however, a question can be found that addresses the interviewee's knowledge or skills, and thus leads to a solution, instead of either a complaint or a plea for sympathy.

■ FOCUSING THE INTERVIEW

The focus of the communications audit process is behaviour, not attitude. If there are systematic, factual issues that can be changed by the decisions of executives, then these are legitimate subjects for scrutiny and, if they check out through triangulation, for recommendations. Such matters are not dependent on likes and dislikes. They are investigated by the questionnaire, and they frequently resurface in detail during interviews wherein the auditor finds out how much emotion surrounds, for example, some inequality (or perceived inequality) in the way people are treated.

Interviews must be based on information, that is, facts. Often to the people in the organization, much appears to be solely personality based. From the auditor's vantage point outside the interaction of personalities, he or she can see the generic, predictable patterns that are at work. For instance, suggestions may be heard that a supervisor prefers some employees to others, abrogates policy decisions, or makes arbitrary judgements. If the auditor recognizes that this person is in the gatekeeper position at the junction of a Y in the communication network, and what is more has not been given any systematic way of distinguishing among the messages that he or she must reroute, then the auditor can see that this is not a personality problem but a structural problem, and thus is accessible to rational solution. As long as the problem is seen in terms of personality, then all solutions are drastic, and tend to take the form of statements such as: 'We'll have to get rid of him, he's not doing his job'. If the job can be reanalyzed and broken down into its components with respect to communication, then there are non-threatening alternatives.

In the hypothetical case of the person at the Y fork, his or her input to the analysis is essential to solving the problem. The auditor must find out what kinds of message are rerouted, on what basis, with what frequency, and with what effects. The impersonal information from the network study will corroborate what the auditor is told. From the person him or herself, the auditor can often find out what they would do to cure the problem, although this suggestion may come indirectly.

Statements such as, 'I need three more hours in each day', are revealing because they point to a variety of solutions the auditor might offer that include finding an assistant, rerouting information before it gets to the person at the Y, or establishing a simpler method of prioritizing. In any case, discovering what it is that the people next in the chain want to know will almost certainly be useful. This information can be obtained from questionnaires, surveys and also through subsequent interviews. However, if the auditor becomes emotionally involved with the person in the middle of the problem, either championing or decrying the personalities involved, it is impossible to reach an effective solution, or for that matter for the auditor to be useful to him or her.

■ PROGRAMMING THE INTERVIEW

The interview itself should be simple and objective. The auditor should note the following:

(a) Start by establishing formal designations: the 'name, rank and serial number' information. This includes the person's:

- job title;
- reporting relationships (how many report to him or her, to whom he or she reports);
- functions, responsibilities, tasks;

(b) Write down what people say in the order they say it, playing back to them their own words and phrases as notes are taken.

(c) Ask for expansion and clarification. (Resist the temptation to phrase this, 'And what do you *really* do?' even though this is in fact what is being requested.) The auditor is looking for:

- *tasks*, this time in detail, with examples (prompt: how often? how many? who helps you?)

- *project/task*, specific responsibilities with examples (prompt: who shares responsibilities? who replaces you if you're sick? what would happen if you left?)
- *planning responsibilities* (prompt: how do you contribute to the overall purpose of the organization?)

(d) Ask the interviewees ways in which they would improve things if it were up to them. A non-threatening way of asking this question is, 'If you had a magic wand and could do anything you liked with this organization, what would be your three wishes?' This question also has the value of eliciting a sense of the person's attitude. Occasionally, people reply by saying 'I'd blow the whole thing to kingdom come', and then quickly force a laugh or say, 'Not really'. These verbal give-aways are useful to notice and remember. If it turns out that several people make the same kind of negative slip, and yet go on to tell how wonderful everything is, or how well they are doing personally, or how the real problem is somewhere else in the environment, the economy or the relationship with the government or regulating agency or supplier . . . etc., then the auditor should be well aware of the fact that there is something not being told because people cannot bear to put it into words.

These are the 'organizational secrets' that are indirectly concerned with the problems. The auditor should not burst into speech and reveal that he or she has noticed a significant gap in someone's conversation, especially if they don't want to admit that they're unsure about the future of the company, or the succession to a soon-to-be vacant job, or hearsay of a merger, or an impending restructuring of products or services. The auditor's job is not to sympathize, but to solve the problem by pin-pointing what information is needed, from whom it should come, and by what channel it should arrive at its destination.

(e) Listen to the grumbles which surface during interviews, both for their content and for Maslow's insight that a grumble indicates what people really need (*see:* page 187).

For example, a communication auditor may cause someone to talk at length about his concern about mis-spellings in memos. At first, the auditor might be tempted to say, 'It really doesn't matter whether people use US or British spelling, so long as the memos are understandable'. Not only will this reaction alienate the interviewee, it will mean that the auditor has missed at least two possibilities. Perhaps the person is looking for the *prestige* of being able to impose his will in this very minor matter, or perhaps he wants the *sense of belonging* conferred by everyone conforming to the same norms. Once again, neither approve nor disapprove, but ask for some factual way out of the problem such as, 'Would you accept majority rule on the subject?', 'Would you prefer a direct order from senior management?' or, 'For how many people is this a problem?'

(f) Keep to the factual. It is important that interviews attend to communication that has organizational validity – the objective, necessary interactions which make an organization work. If the interview can be focused on such factual matters, the interviewees will give more than an insight into the human, non-logical, intuitive and emotional side of personalities, rituals, traditions and the like, they will also tell how these personal problems can be solved by systematic intervention that does not undermine anyone's individuality.

When interviewing a number of people it is necessary to have a protocol or guiding list of questions to help keep attention on the factual. (Look at the sample interview protocol on page 149.) A good technique is to have a copy of the protocol for each meeting, and to tick off the questions as they are answered, not worrying if one or two are omitted as the conversation flows from topic to topic. Then, at the end of the interview, the auditor can check the list and pick up what was missed. Notes follow the natural movement of the conversation, protocol provides you with a checklist. When preparing for the next interviewee, the auditor may want to highlight certain questions in the protocol that have been exposed as important by previous interviewees.

(g) Use a tape recorder, only if the interviewer and interviewee agree. There is no hard and fast rule about the use of a tape recorder. The auditor's preference, modified by the reaction of the interviewees, is the best guide. A tape recording ensures accuracy, but it can also be threatening. The perception of the interviewee is important, but what is at issue is not so much the recording, but the trust in the auditor as a responsible person who will respect confidences. People will say, 'I'd rather you turned that thing off', and others will accept it without objection. The auditor should not make an issue out of using or not using the recorder, and whether or not it is used, the auditor should take notes. If a recording is made, notes will save time; if not, they are the only way of refreshing memory.

(h) Use some of the questions from the survey. This allows the auditor to gain more detail, since people will often talk freely when they will refrain from writing.

(i) Always wrap up the interview with thanks, but before doing so, ask some version of the last question in the protocol (*see:* page 149). Variants might be: 'Is there anything that you expected me to ask which I haven't?' or 'Is there anything you feel that I've missed?' or 'Has this interview raised any questions or comments you would like to share with me?' Any such question puts the responsibility for completeness into the interviewee's hands.

■ ADDITIONAL NOTES

Interviews can produce direct oppositions and contradictions. Organizations contain contradictions without difficulty: however, if they become oppositions between two people who espouse different versions of what the facts are, then they must be unravelled by some systematic intervention. The interview is *not* the time or place for intervening: that comes later with the report. Unlike the focus group, where consensus is to be generated if at all possible, the interview should not be a means of co-opting people to any point of view, but rather a chance for each interviewee to state his or her case as force-fully as he or she wishes. The auditor's role is not to debate, but to ensure that he or she understands. Reconciliation of conflicting testimony comes later.

Obviously, if an auditor is going to quote an interviewee, it should be with his or her full permission and understanding. Usually, some things are strictly off the record, some are not for attribution, and some are opinions which the interviewees are anxious to have to their credit. Seeing the comments and suggestions by other people that have been put on charts around the room often has the effect of encouraging interviewees to find a useful contribution. It can also make people aware that they are not unique in having a feeling, opinion or wish.

Each person faces the challenge of whether or not to make a statement that can be pinned up on the wall charts. As interviewer, the auditor should encourage positively rather than coerce. However, interviews should never become too relaxed. The auditor should be prepared to go on until an answer is found when there is prevarication or obscuring of an issue or fact. The auditor should distinguish clearly in his or her own mind the difference between being ingratiating (which is inappropriate) and being fair and analytical (which is what he or she is being paid for).

Interviews are much more than opinion or fact-gathering sessions. They can improve the communications climate by fostering the perception that something is being done which is worth doing and in which everyone is invited to contribute.

■ THE CASE STUDY CONTINUES

Jan 20, 21 Interviews

Now that two days of interviewing are over, I see a pattern in the pages of notes I have taken.

Two themes: the separateness of the sections, and the remoteness of upper management. Everyone knows what he or she is doing today, but they're aware that there are changes in the wind, and they all have different notions of what might happen, ranging from the enthusiastic to the depressed. Fortunately, there doesn't seem to be apathy: everyone wants to be here – and not just because they get paid.

Highlights and insights

Franks *(Production)* told me about a piece of equipment that exemplifies what the firm is moving into. Regal has its competitors, but Franks thinks their new products are best. He told me about it factually, simply and with an undercurrent of pride that made me revise my opinion of Franks. I still don't warm to him as a human being, but I can see why he and Lisa Fremden get along: they're dedicated to doing whatever they do well.

Michael Worsley *(Sales)* came close to exasperating me. There's a quality of complaining in his voice when he talks about his section that gets on my nerves. However, when I got him to say what they actually do, it was as if another person appeared, and I realized why he is head of sales. He talked about the machine tools aspect of the business with the same kind of enthusiasm for quality that characterizes Fremden and Franks, but in Worsley's case, it's much more dramatic. He can make you care that the machining is done to a finer tolerance than any other company. The problem is that he hasn't found time to learn about the new lines, and he is afraid of seeming ignorant. This isn't good, because he is a potential link between the industrial applications and the high, electronic technology. My guess is that he's over-awed by Fremden and her high-tech wizards.

Daniel Scanlon *(Marketing)* is another link that isn't connecting. He should be joining the buyers to the designers, and focusing the efforts of the sales force. Why did they separate Marketing from Sales? I found out. Daniel was promoted as a bright young man, but couldn't be put over Worsley. So they created Marketing, and essentially limited both of them.

Scanlon knows what he needs: figures from Sales and understanding of what Design can do. The first requires a system, not his two or three increasingly frustrated attempts to get the information from Worsley, who was always too busy. The second requires Fremden to come out of the clouds of what might be done and focus on what the market needs are. Scanlon has been doing his homework, and knows the best forecasts about what's going to be needed. He could do still better if he had data-bank access. He's been working from a personal library of trade and technical magazines that the company should really have supplied to him. He's a gold-mine of information that Fremden doesn't even know exists.

Joe Bailey *(Transportation) is so nice, that it's difficult to realize that his section has some real problems. He should have computer access to transportation timetables – air, sea and land. Right now, they flip through huge books and then have to recheck everything by phone. He didn't even seem to know that all this is accessible through a computer hookup like the one in any travel agency. His staff would do anything for him, but that means that they don't tell him that there's a better way.*

Ben Wills *(Accounting) is the systems man. Knows the VP personally, but is meticulous about not having this be seen as a clique. (This seems to be a general paranoia, I don't know why. Perhaps it was a problem once, but now it's an avoidance-mechanism that excuses all sensible informal interactions. It's the inverse of what's so often the case: they are all trying to be formal, as if it were a sin to consult informally.) Wills, I think, could write a large chunk of my report better than I, because he is more generally knowledgeable than anyone else about the company. But he's quiet, almost withdrawn, and his combination of silence and ability means that he inherits all the work nobody else wants.*

I had this brainwave after he left: put him in charge of the internal communication system. His intelligence is more than adequate, and planning doesn't require oratory.

More about King as leader: he's developed some myths around him. There were allusions to King having been in the Coast Guard as a young man and apparently he helped break up a smuggling ring. I expect the stories have grown in the telling, but that's the type of hero-worship that accounts for King's being trusted.

Mike Wiggins *(Production) is in his low thirties, and regards himself as one of the 'old gang' because he supports King and started out running a lathe before going back to school to study electronics. What I discovered from him is that there are people who have been taken on recently who are not believers in the King legend, and they want rationality, or at least something more than to be told to take the future on trust.*

Carlo Santini *(Production) is a member of the newly-electronified segment of Regal. Once he became aware that I was neutral, he unbent and told me how exasperating some of the 'old gang' can be, and I began to sympathize. The reason for the coast guard vessel in King's picture (which Santini has never seen) became clear: more than an accidental number of older Regal men (notably in Production) have at some time worked for the navy or the coast guard, or have family links to those who do. This gives a paramilitary quality to their dealings with the CEO that is inimical to many of the younger men and women. At best they regard this behaviour as laughable, at worst, tradition-bound and unprogressive. Santini has nothing against King, indeed he likes him. It is the steadily diminishing number of old-style metalworkers who he represents that Santini objects to. I asked him how he'd feel in their shoes,* *and his own answer seemed to surprise him: he hadn't thought about how threatened such people must feel.*

Mariella Comeau *(Transportation) was something of a disappointment. She sang the praises of her co-workers, how much they did, how often they stay overtime, how much they like each other. When I asked her about computerizing part of what Transportation does, her reply was, 'I don't know about that', in such a tone of voice as to make it clear that she didn't want to.*

Ethel Walters *(CEO's Secretary) came heralded by epithets like 'the dragon lady', and 'the grey presence', but away from her post outside King's door, she seems to lose any forbidding quality. We went straight to facts, and the answers fell out simply and effectively. She's the bottleneck between seven people and King, the man they report to. She's also senior secretary, responsible in an unofficial but time-honoured fashion for all the secretarial staff. She ties with Ben Wills for being the most knowledgeable person about the history and functions of the company.*

It was from her that I found out how it is that everyone likes, respects and trusts King. This has been puzzling me, since I could find no reason for it – that is, no communications reason. He apparently confides in nobody, sees managers only one-to-one, is away a lot and even seems to prefer some of his staff, such as Fremden, to others. Yet nobody had anything but good to say about him in the interviews and questionnaires. I had begun to wonder if the question had been misunderstood. Now I suspect that the relatively high number of incompletes on this question are significant in themselves.

It turns out that King is a practitioner of 'management by wandering around'. Every few days or so, he leaves his office, saying 'Just going for a stroll, Ethel', and starts to wander around and talk to people. Everyone gets talked with at least once in every six months. King knows the names of children and girlfriends, the sick mothers, the uncles with arthritis, the newlywed daughters – the lot. To meet him, I'd never have expected it, because he came across to me at first as a remote workaholic.

A part of this mystique is Ethel Walter's doing. She keeps a book of birthdays, anniversaries and other significant dates for King, and he looks at it before he takes his 'strolls'. She covers for him more than most secretaries, and that makes up for areas where he should be more knowledgeable. His public relations talents with his staff do not extend to, in fact they avoid his managers! According to Ethel Walters, he thinks of them as able to look after themselves.

Shelley Peters *(Communication/Marketing). Shelley and I finally took the plunge of objectifying our relationship to be the same as everyone else. This isn't easy because she has strong ideas of what she wants out of the audit, and yet knows that she must let it take its course. She wants to do more with The Regal Report, her newsletter, and also knows how to do it. Her problem is the tortuous path to finished copy. Not only does she have the usual* problems with getting the text approved by King, who always seems to have more important things to do, but she also has to pour the entire typing and editing through the 'typing pool' arrangement of word processors in Accounting, seldom getting the same operator two days running. She's frustrated by this situation, and hungry for her own computer with laser printer.

Shelley is so totally misplaced in Marketing that everyone tries to ignore it. Oddly, I'm not so sure. If she worked with Marketing and Design, she could be the bridge I'm looking to build between those two departments, and that could grow naturally into Sales. Scanlon puts her off, possibly because he feels threatened; Worsley in Sales is impossible to deal with, and the more she speaks to Fremden, the less the other two will deal with her.

The face-to-face style that King has generated with his troops has backfired among the managers: they never meet formally, and they watch each other like hawks to see who's talking to whom – as do their staff. Result: a reluctance to interact.

J. B. King (CEO) took more than half an hour to poke around my office and ask me questions. Thank goodness I'd spent some time updating my charts and notes on the wall. When we sat down, I was at a disadvantage from having responded to **his** questions from the moment he walked in the door. I began by asking him how many people report to him. He avoided the question, so I had to face him with the fact that seven managers and two VPs report to him one-to-one, never as a group. I went a little further than non-directed questioning, and kept asking him until he gave the answers I was looking for: he hates going nine-to-one (seven heads, two VPs), and even avoids group work beyond twos and threes. From then on, it was time to pull back and let Rogerian process take over. I confronted him with himself several times: the fact that he has great plans, but doesn't share them; the fact that he doubts everyone will upgrade to new standards, but that he doesn't do any staff training. He winced when he saw that he had a contradiction to deal with that he had made himself. 'I'll have to think about that', he said several times. Then he told me to ignore Maintenance and Shaughnessey. 'We'll be making a new arrangement. Just pretend he's not there.' I was on the point of demanding to know why, but he got away on me.

After all the nice things I heard about King, I feel almost as if I had just been court-martialling the Archangel Gabriel. No. If he's good enough to put together a company like this one, then he has to learn a few things I can teach him about how to make it work.

Chapter 9
CONTENT ANALYSIS

Content analysis concentrates on the question 'What are they writing about?' by examining the records that the organization keeps.

Content analysis examines paper. Memos, letters, rule books, order forms, minutes of meetings, newsletters, job descriptions, office guidelines – anything that is committed to paper as a part of the business of running an organization. In practice, this can generate a great deal of material, indeed, much more than can be read by the auditor in the limited time available. What is more, a great deal of what is written is concerned with things that happened long ago and are no longer relevant. However, these documents are the recorded history of the organization – or at least the raw material out of which history can be understood and made relevant to the present.

An auditor is not a historian, even though some of the methods of the study of history are applicable to communication auditing. Where a historian might search for years, looking for an unusual fact buried in the files, an auditor is interested in the typical, the regular and the routine rather than the exceptional. Thus the auditor can (and indeed must) sample intelligently to discover the answer to a question to which very few people can respond accurately: 'What are the organization's routines?' In general, people reply by telling what was *unusual* today or this week, simply because routine becomes invisible to those who are involved in it. Paper, that is, records and files, can give answers because they can be sifted and sorted independent of the passions of the moment or the enthusiasms of those who were involved. The repetitiveness of routine can be examined, counted and assessed. Evaluating records on paper provides a counterbalance to interviews and other instruments, all of which tend to focus on what is at the forefront of people's minds where they keep current issues and problems.

In order to avoid crippling boredom, content analysis has to be selective; however, the selection process has to be objectively acceptable to the organization, or results will not be believed. Someone will spring up and say, 'But you didn't look at *this*', and on that one exception build an edifice of distrust. To avoid this happening, agree what is relevant, what is exceptional and what is generic at least in general terms with the appropriate people. (This has another value: if the auditor is a newcomer to the organization, some issue of considerable importance to the culture of the firm might otherwise be missed.)

■ THE 80/20 RULE OF THUMB

The communications auditor is attempting to distinguish the 80 per cent routine from the 20 per cent unusual paperwork, in order to speed up the former and improve the latter. On the one hand the auditor is trying to simplify, on the other to ensure that a proper level of concern and participation is accorded to unusual or important matters. Above all, it is important to distinguish the two kinds of paperwork so that others may do so too.

Content analysis must be objective for another reason as well: it is an aspect of the audit which can (and usually should) be done by assistants. It is not desirable that the auditor be the person who reads all the way through the foot-high pile of memos; it is only necessary that the auditor has a demonstrable theory about what is going on in those memos, and also some suggestion as to how to improve it.

The secret of effective content analysis is the selection of what has to be counted and measured. The simpler the items selected, the more effective will be the analysis – provided the auditor selects appropriately.

The classification system should profile the written activities of the organization, and should be capable of being expressed in the form of a table. The headings might include the 'routine but individually unique' messages with a frequency per day, per week or per month. This is the kind of information on the basis of which written communication can be policed and redirected to more effective channels to the betterment of the organizational communication practised by the firm.

■ STEP ONE: THE FIRST CUT

Accordingly, the auditor should carry out a 'first cut' involving a survey of a randomly selected, relatively brief period of a day, or at most a week. If care is taken not to choose the week of the CEO's vacation, Christmas week or the week of the annual stock taking, there is every chance that the auditor will get a profile of what is happening routinely within the organization. From this experience, a short list of sensitive or problematic communications can be drawn up so that any similar events can be recognized and added to the list. These key subjects, chosen from *both* the 80 per cent routine and the 20 per cent unusual classifications (not more than a dozen, often fewer) then become the sorting boxes for a more careful analysis of the organization's paper. A fresh classification can be added if this becomes necessary, or over-large classifications can be broken down into separate issues. Items from the 20 per cent of unusual paperwork class may deserve individual attention.

■ STEP TWO: CLOSE ANALYSIS

The auditor should choose a week (or if there is relatively little material, a month), and examine the available paper for that period. It may be necessary to expand (or collapse) categories from the 'first cut'. This step can be done by assistants.

Sample categories for content analysis

Each piece of paperwork should be classified according to the following categories.

By subject at issue
Product or service description (new, proposed, cancelled, competing, etc.)
Personnel (hiring, firing, promoting, disciplining; job descriptions, grievances, etc.)
Administrative (procedures, policies, rules, advisories, etc.)
Planning (new product lines, future direction of organization, etc.)
Customers/clients (complaints, suggestions, market surveys, queries, requests, etc.)
Suppliers (complaints, suggestions, alternatives, etc.)
Accounting (bills, receipts, orders, invoices, payroll, etc.)
Government (taxes, payroll deductions, regulations, etc.)
In addition, each instance should be coded:

By type of communication
Memos, letters, reports, studies, proposals, etc.

By source
Who sent it?

By destination
Who received it?

By action taken
What happened? (And who made it happen?)

■ STEP THREE: EVALUATION

Now the auditor must evaluate the results. As a result of the first two steps, a matrix can be drawn up on a large sheet of paper from which patterns can be analyzed. The auditor may need to computerize results, but with many organizations the patterns will emerge clearly without the need for heavy duty analysis. No one set of categories will fit all organizations, since each has a different characteristic paper flow. Overlap among classifications is inevitable, and the auditor will have to decide whether this is an unusual problem, or whether the organization has routinely solved it. Some categories can be collapsed, some demand further classification into subsets, and some prove to be better handled as 'other'.

■ WHAT WILL THE RESULTS SHOW?

The results should be able to help tell the organization what can be done to improve written communication in terms of:

● media
● frequency
● clarity and style

Media

The criterion here is appropriateness. The auditor should ask 'Is this the best way of handling this subject?' For example, a disciplinary memo might well be better handled one-to-one; a social memo through the newsletter; a frequently repeated instruction by a standard form; one line of advice to someone next on shift work by a log book, etc.

Information technology
Content analysis overlaps with the technology assessment discussed in Chapter 10. A great deal of paper based internal messaging can be replaced by 'electronic mail' or interlinked computers. The more repetitive the activity, the more appropriate it is to computerization; particularly if there is a scheduling aspect to the problem where many people have to work together to accomplish tasks by certain deadlines.
Electronic messaging is:

● fast;
● not dependent on the participants' physical presence;
● certain ('I didn't get your message' is not an acceptable excuse)

In addition, electronic messaging can be

● one-text and up-to-date (when several people contribute to a scheduling problem there is no question of 'which version?');

- protected against operator interference (for example, a travel agent cannot alter the assigned schedules or fares);
- either universal (to all points) or individually addressed;
- intercompatible with clients, customers, suppliers, shippers, etc., *if* the appropriate system is chosen.

There are also a number of electronic messaging options other than computers that can solve problems of frequency and appropriateness.

- The electronic noticeboard in a heavily used place (such as a cafeteria) is a relatively inexpensive way of handling important, routine but not regular events such as 'Stock-taking starts on Monday', or the news about a staff party.
- The phone-message recorder can be used to give daily instructions or information when there is no, or little need for interactive conversations.
- Tele-conferencing can replace endless letters or meetings involving costly travel. However, it is a multiple communications tool that requires special study to be cost-effective, since there are so many versions, including: slow-scan video, full action video, interactive computers, electronic 'chalkboards', full interaction with voice and video, video one way telephone the other, etc.

Frequency

Communication frequency has to be examined from *both* the point of view of the receiver and of the sender. It is very easy for people in an organization to forget that their routine may well be someone else's unusual event. This problem can be summarized by recording the kind of reaction caused by a failure to understand the other person's point of view: 'After ten years of working for this organization, Accounting gets the computer to send me a form. I think I deserve a personal letter, an interview, at least a telephone call from a human being.' Frequently, the person who sent the offending message deals with several such items each month, and regards them as routine.

The communications auditor should examine the newsletter, the office manual, the letter system (particularly when letters are circulated), and office-forms from invoices to requisition slips (being careful not to overstep into the proper concerns of financial auditors and accountants). Simple frequency counts will tell a great deal about the organization, whether or not the auditor chooses to comment upon or suggest improvements to the written communication system. The auditor's understanding of the routine which lies behind what has been told in interviews will be immeasurably enhanced, and he or she will probably see a great deal more of the 'iceberg' that lies underwater – or in less metaphoric terms, the everyday life of the organization which is so ingrained as to be invisible to its members.

The auditor and his or her assistants will need to prepare tables setting out what has been observed, so that it is possible to describe the data in the final report with sentences such as:

'On an average week, this firm processes 128 invoices, answers 8 letters to prospective clients, responds to 15 requests from new or potential clients who have called in person or by phone and who need written materials, sends 11 memos addressed to more than one person and 2 between individuals, processes 65 requisitions internally, orders 45 items externally (with supporting internal documents) and fills in 3 government forms.'

This may well be news to senior management, simply because they have never thought in these terms, and are wondering vaguely why they can never seem to get their reports typed by constantly occupied secretaries.

Clarity and style

Style and content are not separate: how things are said affects total meaning. This marriage of style and content can be investigated by asking whether there are repeated metaphors. For example:

- *sports or warfare metaphors:* team playing; defensive measures; game plans; offensives;
- *sexual metaphors:* consummation of deals; wooing the client;
- *jargon:* impacts; down-the-road possibilities; on line; on-going; state of the art; high tech.

Of themselves, these are merely the inadvertent choice of words by individuals: taken as a whole, they can be an objective clue to the corporate culture of the organization. In some cases, they can be proof of an attitude or posture which is so ingrained as to be invisible. If the auditor says, 'This organization is geared towards sports and very macho-masculine in its communications', the CEO and board may say that the auditor is over-sensitive – particularly if the point is that female employees are systematically and invisibly given second class status. On the other hand, if the auditor can point to a content analysis which shows an overwhelming fondness in written communication for sexist or at least sexual metaphors, the point will stand a better chance of getting a hearing, and the corroborative evidence from surveys and interviews will be the more solidly based.

When the auditor considers longer written materials such as mission statements, reports to and from clients, internal planning documents, occasional papers and the like, it should first be agreed what is being looked for. Since these are not repetitive or routine, what can be learned from them may well be *other than* content – matters such as how to organize the typing, revising, editing, proofing, and so on. Since the auditor is not likely to be an expert on the content of these documents in that he or she is not an engineer, a planner, an architect, a social worker or whatever, he or she will only be able to supply generic communication information on which good management decisions can be made.

■ THE CASE STUDY CONTINUES

Jan 23 Content analysis preliminary
I'm a bit out of step with my original plan. I only got the content analysis report back today, and it requires work. I set up the protocols for Ted to work on, and he worked his way through a knee-high pile of paper.

The matrix of what gets written, its subject, origin and destination is clear enough. What is a problem is the sheer bulk of documents from Transportation – do they really need that much paper to run their department?

Once again, I am struck by the thought that what this place does is a secret. Everyone knows, but nobody says – least of all in print. Product lists and catalogues are treated as separate and unique items, so are what pass for planning documents. There is no indication of any planning interaction among departments, even when we went looking for drafts or first memos or anything whereby one section could have been exchanging information with another.

Finding out that something doesn't exist is much more difficult than noting down what does. It took some careful questioning of Shelley to get the information gap outlined without her running off to ask questions that would cause instant paranoia among the department heads. The interviews will confirm or deny my growing confidence that my role is to get the heads of departments together with the CEO. If they accept that, they can start working out all the other problems in no time.

That recognition avoids my having to walk all over Shelley for the content of her in-house newsletter, because she's not being told anything beyond social notes and trivia about the building. At present, the nicely-printed, nicely-photographed, competently-written Regal Report is barely worth doing. It could be a steady source of information that really does motivate, but that requires that Shelley gets information that not even the heads of departments know.

This isn't a management audit, but something has to be done about Accounting! I want to break it down so that it is an accounting department, instead of a combination of work, including sending out letters, typing pool and general dogsbody for anything to do with what is the communications officer's job.

A note about style: Ted has turned up a fondness for military – particularly nautical – metaphors. It's not strong enough by itself to make much of in a report, but it's clear that there is navy, or a least maritime, influence here. People 'chart a course', 'muster', 'make heavy weather', and 'come aboard'. At least two people greeted me with 'welcome aboard' when I did my walk-around, although I didn't notice it at the time.

Chapter 10
TECHNOLOGY ASSESSMENT

Technology assessment in the audit process can be considered in three steps.

1. Assessing technology in use
2. Assessing needs
3. Planning new technology implementation

The auditor can help solve problems in all three steps by considering:

- the human contexts that the rest of the audit analyzes;
- the use to which the machines will be or can be put;
- the ways in which the machines will complement or undermine the existing formal and informal communication networks of the organization.

The best approach is to begin by assessing *attitudes* and the willingness of personnel to use new equipment or technology (*usage*).

■ ATTITUDE

Assessing attitude is finding out whether or not people *like* some new gadget or tool. Their satisfaction can be measured as a product of all the individual subjective responses, and described in an organizational context. What is more, people are usually willing to talk about machines more openly and directly than they are about people.

■ USAGE

Usage is the way people *behave* with a gadget or tool. Most electronic machinery can be programmed to count the number of uses, allowing us to observe the way we *actually* behave, independent of attitude. Copiers and word processors will 'count themselves' by the page, the word or even the keystroke; many new telephone systems and all long distance systems count by the call and time, and so on. This fact makes the logging of uses much easier than in other kinds of communication assessment.

However, frequency by itself is nothing: there must also be something to compare to. This can be another similar business; the same organization over different times; or different aspects of the same organization, all of which implies that the auditor must examine (or at least read about) other, comparable installations.

■ STEP ONE: ASSESSING TECHNOLOGY IN USE

The first step in a technology assessment is to sample representative people throughout the organization in order to understand attitudes towards existing equipment. The questions to ask are:

● 'Do you use (name of instrument)?'
● 'Do you like using it?'

Do you use ...?

This question may seem excessively simple but it works. It is important to record the answers verbatim – especially any negative answers. (The auditor should not rely on memory, or summarize into positive/negative, because it is necessary to analyze the actual words of many people.)

Negative responses to the question may include:

1. 'No, my secretary uses it.'
2. 'No, I prefer to do it my way.'
3. 'No, there's too much waiting.'
4. 'No, but I'm planning to when I get the time to learn.'
5. 'No, none of us in this section do.'
6. 'No, I haven't been given a machine of my own.'
7. 'No, I'm too busy.'

It is best *not* to hand out questionnaires with opportunities for people to check off excuses or enthusiasms, because the one that the person offers *first* and unprompted is the clue to his or her attitude. The auditor can keep score on repeated reasons, looking for patterns that can be explained with reference to other attitudes and conduct.

Clearly, each of the foregoing answers implies a different shade of attitude.

1. Could imply that the speaker believes that using the machine is 'beneath him', or 'inappropriate to his or her rank', or that this social distinction makes a good excuse.
2. Could imply that the machinery is inappropriate, or that the person does not know how to use it comfortably.
3. Could imply that more machines, careful scheduling or evaluation of priority are needed.

4. Could imply just what it says, but also could indicate a fear of failure that stands ahead of actually trying.

5. Could imply either that the section is a proud hold-out, or a neglected group.

6. Could be a bid for status, or a way of avoiding learning, or a legitimate problem.

7. Could be (and probably is) a shallow excuse.

Any interpretations must be clarified with further probing questions. Many older people who have not recently received any formal training find it difficult to face learning new skills, particularly when younger, more junior people already possess those skills. The auditor's job is not to psychoanalyze people, but to discover what is needed to solve the problem. The auditor must consider the following points

- Is it technical, that is, is the machine appropriate?
- Is it a simple training problem that can be solved with classes for those who must learn?
- Is it a more complex and psychological problem that requires individualized learning for some people?

Do you like using ...?

This question will elicit suggestions and comments on how to improve the situation. It generates immediately useful material for the report, even if the statements are critical of existing machinery or its use. (Of course, the auditor will not blindly recommend on this basis alone.)

■ STEP TWO: ASSESSING NEEDS

Needs assessment, or deciding what equipment to acquire, is more complicated, since it involves an educated guess as to how well the new equipment will fit into the particular organization. Accordingly, the auditor starts by assessing what *is* (step one), and then moving to examine what *might be*. The auditor can make use of reported behaviour from other, similar organizations. (The source should be reputable magazines, periodicals and books, not propaganda from suppliers of hard or software.)

A satisfactory way of examining both attitude and the way people will probably behave is by convening a technological needs assessment focus group. This approach is founded on the idea that the people who do the job and who will use the machinery should be a primary (though not the only) source of information when assessing needs. (*See* Chapter 5, Focus Groups.)

The technique is to convene a group made up of management (who usually have the decision on what to buy) and staff (who usually end up using the machinery). The simple act of consultation between these two groups can improve the decision-making process and vastly simplify implementation. Sometimes it is necessary to hold two such meetings, one with the user-staff, one with the purchaser-managers. This is particularly necessary if there are already tensions between the two groups.

This approach assumes that there are people in the organization who are aware of what could be done with modern equipment. If this is not the case, the auditor's task is to prepare some material for focus group members to read – articles or parts of books (less than 20 pages in all, if they are to be read) that give generic information on what can be done with computers in different task areas such as accounting, drafting, writing, record keeping and so on. This introduces them to appropriate expectations they might have, and gets them to a level of consciousness necessary for the focus group.

Wants and needs

The first task of a needs assessment focus group is to ask people what they want; the second is to discipline the resulting 'wish list' in the context of constraints and limitations. Third, the list must be prioritized, and subsequently it becomes possible to negotiate a joint approach between those who buy and those who use, that will result in a win-win solution wherein the organization as a whole benefits.

Unfortunately, people tend to want to negotiate first and find out facts later. Thus when facing a focus group on technological assessment, it is essential to start with an uncritical session of brainstorming around the question 'What do you need?' What should then happen is that 'I want statements' should emerge.

Incentives and barriers

After a distinct break or closure of this first stage, it is possible to ask the double-barrelled question: 'What positive forces will help you achieve your needs, and what barriers stand in your way?' The results of this second round of brainstorming will produce a double list of positives and negatives. As moderator, the auditor will have to take people beyond the single concept answer to the barriers side of the question that emerges in one word, 'money'. The auditor can prompt them with some or all of the following concepts:

● training;
● timing;

- organizational factors (in whose department and under whose supervision?);
- compatibility of machinery, both internally and externally;
- job enhancement, loss, change, additions;
- information needs;
- appropriate hard and software;
- available hard and software.

The recorder should have two charts or blackboards to record this two-sided brainstorming. The auditor should avoid getting into the polemics of horror-stories about people being displaced by machines with the simple statement: 'I'm conducting this audit expressly to avoid that kind of thing happening.' (This implies that the auditor must be confident that he or she is telling the truth, which in turn implies that he or she is confident of the rapport with the CEO.)

At the close of this stage, when people have started to re-examine rather than offer new ideas, they will characteristically want to start negotiating. Again they must be held back from getting ahead of themselves.

They now have the negatives and the positives, the desires and the constraints. Now they must assign priorities. The grid in Fig. 10.1 can be a useful way of organizing the data which the group has discovered.

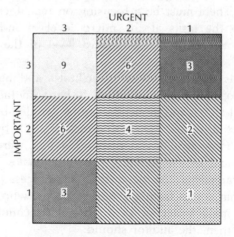

Figure 10.1 A priority grid

The grid allows for consensus by asking each person to prioritize each project on a 1–3 scale of both urgency and importance. For example, it may be very important (3) to have adequate training for those who will use new computers, but it is not urgent until the computers arrive (2). The product (6) of the two puts training people on a higher priority than developing new in-house software, which might have an importance value of 3 but an urgency of 1, yielding a product of 3. If several people have different values, it is possible to distinguish time from severity – factors that frequently are amalgamated by people who then compare and argue vehemently for priorities that have differing components.

The auditor should avoid taking a vote by adding up all of the priority scores and dividing by the number of people in the room: what is required is reasoned and reasonable understanding of *why* the priorities are thus, not a forced agreement that may be seen later as a negotiator's trick.

The process of prioritizing also makes it possible for the auditor to encourage staff to suggest strategies for change. This introduces the negotiation phase without (or with minimum) adversorial spirit. With any luck at all, the negotiation is characterized by finding joint solutions, setting group approved goals, and accepting and sharing responsibilities.

The entire process is largely a matter of harmonizing perceptions. Management may have the perception that staff wants and wishes are impossibly expensive; staff may have the perception that management is interested only in holding on to its power, or even using machines to replace people. There must be a focusing on real, fact-based agendas which relate to the tasks at the micro level of individual acts of communication as well as at the macro level of the mission of the organization.

To achieve this goal, the auditor as facilitator and intermediary must encourage appropriate language which is hard on facts and soft on people. Personal attack and innuendo can be avoided by asking people to clarify in factual terms, ('Does this mean . . .?'), by turning questions around, ('How would you respond if you were in his or her position . . .?), and by encouraging people to make 'We statements' rather than 'I statements'. At the close of the process, there should be an agreement that comes from a group of people who feel themselves to be united to make better use of a particular technology.

In summary, then, the auditor should:

- establish perceived needs;
- identify positive forces and negative barriers;
- assign priorities;
- suggest mutual strategies for change;
- establish goals, share responsibilities, make commitments.

■ STEP THREE: MANAGING NEW TECHNOLOGY IMPLEMENTATION

Technology assessment can also be a way of preparing the organization for what happens when and if it adopts certain information/communication instruments.

The factors involved are:

1. Perceived needs
2. Expert opinion on needs
3. Expert opinion on hard and software
4. Organizational impact
5. Training

1. Perceived needs

In addition to the suggested focus group, questionnaires, surveys, interviews and volunteered suggestions are all possible sources of what the organization perceives as its communication technology needs. In all cases, questions that point to generic needs should be asked rather than individual wants or specific 'brand name' machines.

2. Expert opinion on needs

This is the field of the auditor who must focus all he or she has learned from the audit on the question, 'How could appropriate communication equipment improve this organization?'

To this end the auditor should ask him or herself the following questions about channels of communication.

- Could it be done via another channel? For example, could the present system of internal paper transactions (memos, instructions, etc.) be replaced by interactive computers?
- How much will it cost in time, money, and retraining? For example, how many terminals at what cost would be required to set up a first phase, second phase or total computerization?
- Will the change enhance the storage and accessibility of information? For example, will information now in central files become available to many people simultaneously? Is this appropriate? How long would it take to insert backfiles into the system? Which ones?
- Will legitimate security be compromised? For example, will company secrets be accessible to anyone sitting at a terminal? How strict will access codes have to be?
- What will be the advantages beyond the replacement of the old system? For example, will the organization be helped by the electronic diary feature of most electronic mail, that speeds appointment making? How much time is presently spent telephoning people who are out? Will such 'extras' as electronic messaging significantly help the organization? To what degree?

- Will the new equipment be compatible with existing equipment? For example, with telephones (internal and external), suppliers' systems and customers' systems.
- How much *cannot* be replaced by the new equipment? For example, will some orders and bills still be manual? (A full answer to this question would include checking with the accountants.)

The auditor should be aware that all of these questions are merely applied common sense, and therefore that other people will be asking them as well. The auditor's advantage is in distance from the situation. The territorial imperative of wanting to get 'my' system that fulfils only one person's or group's needs can thus be avoided.

3. Expert opinion on hard and software
There are a great number of highly competitive salespeople who claim that their brand of 'black box' will solve all imaginable problems. As a result, there are many people who have been attracted by 'high tech' and then later perplexed when the promised results are not forthcoming. Usually this is because while most computers will do many kinds of task, each has a *primary* task that it does best. Some work best on numbers, some on word processing, some on statistical matters, some on accounting, some on graphics, and so on, even though all claim to do all of these functions. The communication auditor should find out from users (rather than salespeople) the hierarchy of tasks that each machine will do, and should remember that this information changes from month to month.

Experienced, independent computer and communication people have long known the adage GI = GO, that is Garbage In = Garbage Out. The expansion of this simple observation can be expressed in a number of corollaries.

- If a technology is used to mask a basic organizational or communication problem, that problem becomes increasingly expensive to solve, and can even prove to be organizationally lethal.
- If buyers don't know what they're doing and saying before they computerize, they'll be worse off afterwards.
- No one brand or type of machine does everything – no matter what the salesmen say. Each system has its strengths and weaknesses.
- Computers 'crash', malfunction, and can cause incredible frustration. They do not, however, 'make mistakes'. This means that the computer cannot be blamed for what people do to it, and also it means that the computer should not be believed blindly as if it were a flawless oracle.

● In five years' time 'the latest thing' in communication hard or software may well be used in applications *other than* the ones for which it is being sold today. (Nobody expected telephones to be used for *internal* communication; TV was originally thought to be limited to entertaining children with puppet shows; computers were not originally expected to be personally owned, and so on.)

None of the foregoing should be taken as an argument for returning to the quill pen and the clay tablet, only as cautions that technological advances alter much more than one might originally expect. Specifically, technological changes alter communication networks and therefore the power structure of organizations.

For example, if an organization installs computer-conferencing for some but not all of its staff, it is predictable that there will be two cliques or networks: of the computerized and the non-computerized, each with its own characteristics. The computerized network will tend to be less responsive to old formal communication and power structures and be characterized by an increase of generalism, while the uncomputerized network will tend to hark back to a hierarchical system with many specialized functions limited one to a person.

The consequences for the communication climate and corporate culture of the organization can be far-reaching, particularly if the internal split between computerized and the uncomputerized is not healed.

4. Organizational impact

Bringing new machines into the workplace always affects the organization and its power structure. Someone gets to be the chief operator, someone else to be manager responsible, and these new duties are sources of control, and hence of power. Putting it the other way around, people will be chosen to run or manage the machinery and those who are not may well feel unconnected and powerless as a result. Resentment grows under such circumstances, whether or not it is justified. Gossip flourishes, the most prevalent being some version of the statement, 'They're bringing in machines that are taking away our jobs.' What is more, in some cases this may be true.

The time to confront such questions is *before* the machinery is chosen or acquired, when people at all levels can make intelligent personal plans in harmony with the organization as a whole, negotiating agreements sensibly for training, transfer or even termination.

Copious experience over more than three hundred years shows that keeping new machinery a secret until it is installed is the best possible way of generating serious dissatisfaction and upheaval. Since electronic machines are different from those of the industrial age in that most require highly educated or highly skilled people, reactions are more intense and destructive when management adopts new technology without prior consultation. Once there is fearful us-them antagonism between executives and those they are trying to lead, the consequences can include work stoppages and slowdowns that are blamed on the new machinery.

An auditor is heading off the win-lose battles that might take place. He or she is not a scapegoat for coercive change or unilateral management decision making, and should be very sure that the audit is not going to be used for such nefarious purposes. This is not merely a matter of politics or even ethics: such efforts simply do not work!

5. Training

Training should be planned before equipment is chosen and begun (or at least be organized) before it arrives.

If people are not adequately trained and convinced of the efficacy of the equipment, they will misuse, abuse or *not* use it. Most companies purveying communication equipment offer training as part of their installation costs. However, it is up to the organization that is buying the equipment to ensure that training is taken seriously, and taken by everyone. Although the auditor is not necessarily going to be present for the implementation of new machinery, it can be part of an audit to discover what went right and wrong when the last innovation was installed and so forestall repeated mistakes. It is very likely that what is told that is negative about existing equipment is a direct result of poor planning and inadequate or non-universal training.

There are still people, many of them in senior management, who are highly resistant to 'hands on' use of electronic technology. In part, this is a status-based notion that executives do not have to know skills such as typing. It is also a fear of learning something new in a class that includes subordinates, some of whom will learn quicker.

Nor is this limited to senior management. Fear of failing to learn shows up at all levels of organizations, and has to be systematically neutralized. Similarly, it is necessary to avoid the growth of mystiques, guilds and inappropriate proprietorial expertise – people who say, 'Let me do it, that's my job,' when in fact the equipment should be accessible and usable by everyone.

In the office, there is often the perception that computers will put secretaries out of work, and this fear is not groundless. However, the results of several studies indicate that the average secretary spends less than 20 per cent of her time typing, and the rest organizing, managing and facilitating. In other words, 80 per cent of her efforts will not be replaced by a computer, although the work she does will undoubtedly be enhanced by computerizing – again, provided the change is managed effectively and training is thought of not solely in terms of how to operate the machinery. This is why training must include managers, whether or not they actually learn how to operate a computer. Properly managed, computerization can enhance jobs and create new roles. The alternatives are the loss of useful employees, lowered efficiency, and serious communication breakdown that may take months or even years to redress.

■ THE CASE STUDY CONTINUES

Jan. 27 Technology focus group

I held a few interviews and now I think it's possible to see perceptions of need for better communication and information equipment as a spectrum. At one end, there are the over enthusiastic, who want everything and have no idea of the price – still less the cost-efficiency. At the other end are those who are nervous of computers who would be happier with quill pens. In the middle we find relatively sane people divided into those who know what they want, and those who don't know what they need.

The over enthusiastic here are two of Lisa's staff, one man, one woman, and at least half the younger men in the production end who work with the newer designs.

Half the accounting staff, all of Transportation, most of sales, some of the secretaries are nervous about expanding new technology. (The introduction of word processing was abysmal. The implementer – Daniel Scanlon – thought that word processors were fast typewriters, and organized the system in Accounting, because Ben Wills was capable of making it work. No thought was given to job enhancement, use of the system, filing advantages. He's learned his lesson, I think.)

Lisa Fremden (Design) wants a second CADCAM unit, and will probably get it. She already has three micros in her unit, going the whole time. C. Franks (Production) is teaming with Lisa to get the CADCAM because he gets the CAM side. Together, they'll probably succeed. Ben Wills (Accounting) only wants two micros, and would settle for one, but nobody has offered, and he has difficulty putting himself forward. He realizes that he would be able to do his real job, accounting, more easily and much better with a micro.

Joe Bailey (Transportation) needs computers to cope with the increasing complexity of both transportation schedules and government policies, regulations and rules.

Michael Worsley (Sales) needs to organize his work better. Also needs to be in closer contact with his staff, with the competition, with the firm itself. He's trying hard, but it's all going sour on him because he hasn't got time to do anything but grouse about a) how it used to be in the good old days, and b) how hard his staff work for him.

Daniel Scanlon (Marketing) liked using new technology until one bad experience with the word processors. Now he's afraid to get involved again. But he knows that he needs to be analyzing, surveying, studying, accessing data banks, forecasting – all the things that are better and faster done with electronic help.

The problem is classic: they each want the machine they need to become the standard for everyone else. They started arguing the moment I got them together.

I took them through the focus group exercise, and they started to rationalize their personal wants and needs into group needs and priorities. After a while, they got really keen and suggested three scenarios, distinguished by cost.

The Rolls Royce option is to put a dumb messaging terminal on nearly everyone's desk, and micros for most of the staff, ganging them together in the case of accounting and transportation. Plus, of course, one CADCAM for Design. The Ford option is much the same, only no messaging terminals. (I think that the messaging could be done by two more word processors and a software package to link them all together, but I decided to keep that one to myself until I can look into it.) The Ten Speed Bicycle approach is micros for heads of departments.

We had to leave it at that because none of us knew how much money is available. I shall have to get to King, and soon.

What impressed me was their total agreement with the notion that there wasn't enough interaction among the departments. This means that they don't talk together as a team. King's hints and comments about putting in new systems has alerted them and made them hopeful that there's a magical solution to their problems. I didn't disillusion them. If they know they need to talk, that's half the battle.

I think Joe is beginning to understand his need for technological help. He's not young, and he knows nobody can match his experience, so if someone were able to work with him to do the actual programming and configuring of the system, we'd have a more efficient section and a happier man.

PART THREE

The Audit Report

Chapter 11
INTERPRETING DATA
AND DEALING WITH PROBLEMS

By this stage, the communications auditor will be in the final third of the time allotted to the project. Surveys have been received and processed into numbers; a network analysis has generated graphs, charts and diagrams; the notes from the focus groups and interviews have been winnowed down into recurrent themes and issues. The written materials have been read in sufficient detail for the auditor to understand what is contained in the paper trail left by the organization; and the way in which the organization uses technology has been examined.

Now what does it all mean? And how can it be translated into a comprehensive report and recommendations?

■ BASIC PRINCIPLES TO GUIDE ANALYSIS

It is appropriate at this point to return to first principles and ask 'Why is this audit being conducted?' That is, the auditor must go back and read the detailed brief or contract asking 'What do I and the organization reasonably expect to get out of the process?'

The CEO wants decision-making information that will improve communication, and hence the overall productivity and effectiveness of the organization. Eventually, what the auditor has done translates into profits. This is not a direct cause-and-effect sequence, but part of a system improvement that the auditor's presence has initiated. The auditor may well be perceived as someone who is helping save money, redirecting money, or finding where money went to, and all these are legitimate interpretations of his or her role.

But the auditor will also be seen as a disruption to the power structure of the organization: that mixture of formal and informal, positional and personal ascendancy that people have over each other in an organization. The auditor alters this delicate balance at his or her peril, especially when the situation is under strain.

This is why the auditor should start by writing a brief (one page) description of the organization in an objective fashion, concentrating on its communication structure and performance. Similarly, it is important that information has been collected with all the methodological clarity possible, and that the auditor has compared the different instruments so that nobody can possibly accuse him or her of working from unsubstantiated hunches and intuitions. Every issue can be delineated and expressed in at least three contexts, thanks to the auditor's different approaches. The auditor must be confident of the facts.

However, there are too many facts. To pour out all that is now known about the organization and to state what ought to be done would be to take the organization back to where it was at the beginning: drowning in information, lacking direction, not knowing what was important.

The report must be set out so that it makes distinctions about what is important. This implies *prioritized* recommendations based on evaluated information that stands the test of relevance to the entire system.

■ FIRST AUDIENCE IS THE CEO

The report may be read by a number of people, but the most important is the CEO. He or she is the strongest single factor in the decision-making process that the report initiates. If the CEO agrees, then the recommendations will have a fair chance of being implemented. If the CEO disagrees, then the report will at best be accepted in highly selective part, or more likely, shelved. What is more, selective application of the report will almost always fail to satisfy anyone, because the most important points of the analysis and suggestions did not achieve acceptance.

This is why the auditor must make the analysis and recommendations lucidly clear to the CEO. Otherwise the recommendations will have no basis either for initial acceptance, or for convincing communication to the entire organization, or for effective implementation.

The auditor has the content, knows the audience and should by now have a sense of what the CEO will accept. The medium is a formal report based on a recognizable process.

■ ANALYSIS BY STRENGTHS AND WEAKNESSES

The auditor should begin the analysis by setting down findings in terms of strengths and weaknesses. At first, it is best to brainstorm, not to try to order, prioritize or argue the case. The auditor's notebook should be used, as well as the results of each separate instrument. This activity will probably generate a list that looks something like that in Table 11.1.

Regal Instruments	
Strengths	**Weaknesses**
High commitment to organization, quality of service	Senior management have no formal, regular meetings
Attractive, functional work-spaces	CEO's secretary overworked
Job descriptions at lower levels recently revised	Little written history: no minutes of meetings, no job descriptions for management
Communication officer efficient, able, well-trained	
Informative staff newsletter	Marketing, Transportation, and Regional Offices lack interaction
Sales, Accounting make monthly reports	Only Sales and Accounting make monthly reports
Production, Maintenance, have strong identity, morale	Nobody answers the phone between 12 and 1:30
	Communication officer not used to full potential

Table 11.1 Analysis of strengths and weaknesses

The auditor should then carry out the following:

(a) Draw lines indicating connections. This may have been done even as intuitions about and memories of what was discovered were jotted down.

(b) Ask whether present weaknesses can be turned into future strengths, as in the case of the CEO's secretary who is presently an information bottleneck, even though (perhaps because) she is hard-working, overloaded and ultimately loyal to the CEO and the organization. Given more authority (and less work) she might well be a major force for change.

(c) Order the strengths by potential for positive influence. For example, it is good that there are attractive work spaces, but there is not much more that can be done with this line of thinking save to congratulate the organization on its awareness of environmental factors. (The auditor should not neglect to do this inventory of good things: it makes the acceptance of solutions more likely.) On the other hand, the fact that job descriptions have been recently revised at the lower levels is an idea which may be transferred to the management level, where it is so obviously necessary. Similarly, the presence of a communication officer is a resource to be exploited – especially as it has been noted among the weaknesses that he or she is not being used to full potential. Figure 11.1 illustrates how strengths can be prioritized in terms of the potential they have to influence communication within the organization.

(d) Return to the data from the instruments and reconsider the strengths and weaknesses list from two perspectives, asking: 'What has been forgotten?'; and 'How can I prove my point?'

As notes and results are reviewed, words may seem to spring off the page. For example, among the statements recorded in notes on the focus group was the following quotation, 'We talk in pairs: Sales and Marketing, Finance and Transportation, Manufacturing and Maintenance, and the Regional Offices talk among themselves. We never meet as a single organization.' At the time, the remark did not seem particularly significant; now it is both a corroboration of the network analysis and a powerful suggestion of how to solve the problem. Immediately, it can be seen that the comparison is beginning to pay off. The auditor can *both* quote the result of the focus group *and* demonstrate objectively with the network analysis that the (anonymous, of course) speaker's intuition was literally true.

Strengths by potential for positive influence

- Everyone loyal and respectful to CEO (if he told them his plans, they'd follow him anywhere)
- Strong work-ethic (but a need to improve the way work is organized)
- Information potential within organization (if bottlenecks, isolation of departments can be resolved)
- Trained information handlers exist (CEO's Secretary, Communication Officer, Accounting)
- Abundance of highly-educated, skilled, able people (must learn to work together)
- Acceptance of electronic equipment fair to excellent (must choose, train better at next additions)
- Good work environment (move towards equalization?)
- Good attitude towards pay, benefits (problem with younger women)

Figure 11.1 Strengths organized in terms of potential influence

(e) Order the weaknesses by urgency and severity. (The urgent/ important diagram in Table 11.2 can be used.) For example, it is *urgent* that someone answers the telephone over the lunchbreak, but it is not a *severe* problem to solve. The bottlenecking of information at the CEO's office is much more severe, and will require creative thought to solve.

Urgent	Severe
Telephone at noon	Clarify communication goals
Get Transportation on-line	Create links among sections
Clarify maternity leave policy	Solve bottlenecking
Improve reporting inside Sales	Plan appropriate technology

Table 11.2 The urgency and severity of weaknesses

Essentially the auditor is following the same process as that used with the focus groups – brainstorm, classify, prioritize, negotiate – with the difference that the auditor has to go around and around this same process until a single text can be written that will be accepted by everyone, particularly the CEO. In other words, the foregoing examples are merely the starting point: the auditor needs to examine them and the results from the gathered data to:

● corroborate the findings;
● integrate the results (triangulate);
● document from evidence;
● write logical, consistent arguments.

In distinguishing urgent from severe problems, the auditor will probably discover that once the urgent matters he or she is itching to solve are gathered together apart from the severe problems, he or she will realize it is the severe problems that are the reason for being there, for doing an audit. Chances are, the urgent matters are 'masking problems' that are obscuring issues not nearly as simple to solve as purchasing a telephone recording device or arranging for the receptionist to find a replacement at lunchtime. People in organizations can be selectively blind to these symptomatic problems, because to solve them would be to isolate the real difficulties that are more systemic or inherent in the structure of the organization. This is why they need audits that are more than cosmetic, and it is also why the auditor has spent so much time collecting information that allows him or her to penetrate the deep structure of the organization and prescribe with an understanding of the particular problems of the individual organization.

■ FOUR CLASSES OF RESULTS

Looking back through the instrument results, the auditor will probably discover that there are four classes of results:

1. Very *obvious matters* which arose in the first phases of the audit and which the instruments demonstrate unequivocally from several different points of view.
2. Matters to which the instruments drew attention that might otherwise have been missed – particularly the *opinions* of people within the organization, some of which are the best guide to what is wrong and how to make it right.
3. Truly amazing *revelations* which come from cross-tabulating results and discovering the pin-point sources of particular communication opportunities and problems.
4. Integrated, *systemic problems* and issues that are like a tangle of string in that one aspect of the problem cannot be touched without affecting everything else.

These four classes of information are used to design strategies which will be the recommendations. At this stage, the auditor should not try to write the recommendations themselves. Rather, he or she should imagine the problems solved, and reason backwards from the ideal through *several* different ways of achieving the desired solution, *one of which* will be the recommended method, and the *others* will be stated as alternatives discarded for a variety of reasons.

1. Obvious matters

The chances are that some obvious matters emerged from first discussions with the contact person or the CEO. They are the classic problems: lack of upward or sideways communication, fear of upcoming change, bottlenecked information, communication over- and under-load, specific failures of communication which have engendered a poor communication climate.

Unfortunately, most of these difficulties are rather like the common cold – sooner or later everyone gets one, and there's no generally prescribed cure for it. In other words, the auditor has to give individual reference to the problem within this particular organization, without reference to individual personalities, even though a great deal may well have been expressed in those terms. The skill for which the auditor is being paid is to locate the problem in some way which ensures that no individual person will be victimized, and then to point to a way of solving it. Thus, how the auditor words the analysis is very important. Even the least hint of pointing a finger of blame at an individual, office or group should be avoided: instead, focus on the issue and how it can be resolved.

This is where the ability to research both the generic and the particular of organizational communications comes into play. The auditor may refer to established authorities in communication and management, and also to specific recent articles about highly comparable businesses in the same sector. This way, it can be shown both that theory exists as does recent practice in which someone else has had the same problem, analyzed it and solved it. An auditor should give proof that the situation exists, that it has solutions, that the organization may choose among different solutions, and that a particular solution can be recommended for good reasons.

2. Opinions

Within any organization there are theories and counter theories of what is wrong and how to fix it. Frequently, the contentious issues that separate the two or more 'sides' are not particularly important to an outsider, but serve to maintain a state of feuding inaction over the problem. In interviews and focus groups the auditor will in all probability have encountered these theories and quite possibly also the lively debates that take place among their proponents.

The people in an organization are rarely wrong about the existence of a problem: where the difficulty arises is in the *masking* problem which is the debate on how to fix the problem. The auditor must get to the real, root problem behind the theorizing, opinion making and personality based analysis. The auditor's strength is often that he or she was not there at the time of the great snafu, isn't a member of the emotional camps which have opposed each other ever since, and hasn't committed the organization to one solution that excludes someone else's solution.

The auditor must go back to basic principles on which all the people on the organization can agree. This begins with a clear statement of what the organization is and does, why a search for a mission statement was used as the starting point for focus groups, and why every interviewee was asked what it is that he or she does that contributes to the overall purpose of the organization.

From the inescapable overlap among different opinions that the auditor can see, a statement of these real problems can be constructed. They may be straightforward – no mission statement, no overall identification of priorities, no organizational chart, or one so out of date that it is counter-productive. Such problems can be complicated to solve, even though simple to state. In any case, the auditor has now not only discovered the problem, but thanks to the data collection, also has a resource of local opinions as to how to put it right.

Evaluating theories
The auditor should now consider the various theories to which he or she has been exposed and note the following:

● Wherever there is agreement, use the concept, but make sure it is expressed in neutral words.
● When there is disagreement, invent a third option in which both sides can agree.
● As before, research and reference suggestions: do not expect to be believed just because it comes from the auditor. (More than one auditor has found him or herself creating agreement among warring factions by becoming the common enemy. This approach is not productive, since after the enemy has left, the survivors can get back to fighting each other, and nothing is solved.)

Remaining objective
The auditor's objective is to be the midwife of constructive change. This implies that the organization must be able to believe in the solution. It helps if they see their own opinions and beliefs in the report, and it also helps if they do *not* see (or at least are not asked to believe in) those opinions and beliefs to which they are opposed.

This degree of objectivity on the part of the auditor is crucial. This is *their* organization. It is not necessary that the auditor likes the solutions: it is very important that the organization does. Of course, the auditor will attempt to lead people towards humane, modern, effective communications management, and of course the auditor will not recommend anything which is inimicable to his or her conscience or judgement, but it may be necessary that an organization progress through several stages before it reaches the point where the auditor might like it to be.

This is particularly seductive in terms of style, which may mask the more important, systemic problems. The auditor may dislike certain organizational patterns of speech and behaviour such as calling secretaries 'girls', or obsessive protection of very minor status symbols such as named parking places. However, it is important not to call attention to such surface level symptoms, but to try to prescribe for the more serious communication problems. In so doing, the organization will move closer to changing surface level manifestations of the deeper problems. What is more, the auditor will only be thought of as an over-sensitive worrier if he or she calls attention to such problems, and the report will cause irritation when it should generate understanding.

3. Revelations

Let us suppose that the auditor is examining the response to survey questions concerning the benefits package. The overall average comes out at a bland three on a Likert scale of one to five, and it is difficult to see anything significant in such vanilla results. In a fit of imaginative brilliance, the auditor cross-tabulates the responses with the demographics of the organization (section, rank, length of service, sex). The results are amazing.

All the people over 45 (about one sixth of the organization) are nervous and upset lest they lose their 20 years of pension contributions; and all the women between 25 and 35 (about one quarter of the women) are concerned what might happen to their jobs should they become pregnant. The other people in the organization do not have these concerns, and their majority opinion has masked the problems.

Company benefit plans are not subjects that surface meaningfully in focus groups or interviews, and they are usually ignored within the daily round of work. Nonetheless, they are issues that can generate resentment, hostility and fear, negatively influencing communication and work as a whole.

The most important thing about these revelations is that they are usually news to the management of the organization, and are frequently greeted with enthusiastic responses because they are so easy to deal with. The usual response is 'We didn't know!' when the auditor provides such particular examples of communication failure.

The solution to these problems is usually quick, relatively inexpensive and highly effective in exorcising a great deal of negativity which may have built over the years. Incidentally, the auditor will impress the organization by pointing out something of which it was unaware, and it may then be easier to engender belief in the solutions to more contentious and complicated issues.

4. Systemic problems

The medical metaphor for communication audits applies particularly strongly with systemic problems which question the very nature of the organization's structure. It is relatively easy to deal with surface symptoms, but more difficult to choose ways of affecting the deeper difficulties that permeate the organization. This is because the problem is like a coin, one side of which is a positive factor while the other is negative. Somehow, the auditor must separate the two sides of the coin and offer alternative courses of action that will not destroy the organization's strengths while solving its weaknesses.

In practice, all four kinds of analytical situation emerge from the instruments, each requiring a different approach when the auditor comes to set out the report. The auditor should not be surprised if the very obvious matters that struck him or her at first turn out to be systemic. However, it is important to make sure that every possible connection from the obvious surface symptom to its underlying causes have been traced.

The systemic problems – frequently only one is all it takes – are the main focus of the report. They, and the auditor's solution, must be expressed in such a way that senior management *want* to make the necessary changes in the way they do business, and are confident that the results of their altered behaviour will ripple through the organization, making it more efficient and productive.

■ BUILDING ACCEPTANCE

The report must build acceptance as it analyzes and recommends. The auditor should consciously employ the same techniques used in doing the research. These are:

1. Triangulated results
2. Diplomatic choice of terms
3. System-based approach
4. Sensitivity to corporate culture

1. Triangulated results

There is another class of analytic result which comes from the cross-comparison (triangulation) of different methodologies and instruments. The auditor has been using this technique from the beginning, letting one instrument inform another, but now he or she may write sentences such as: 'Alerted by the response to survey questions dealing with information flow, we asked a cross-section of employees to comment on inter-departmental communication, and as a result saw that information about day-to-day changes in product scheduling was not reaching all the relevant departments in a timely fashion.' (The auditor might want to be blunter or gentler in expression of this problem, depending on the evaluation of the CEO: but in any event, the auditor must above all be clear.)

The auditor should then itemize the possible solutions. These could include:

● computerize, provide on-line information (expensive);

- memo changes in scheduling (slow, no feedback);
- departments circulate 'daily report' (slow, hard to enforce);
- all heads of departments meet daily (too frequent);
- all heads of departments meet weekly (recommended).

When set out in this way, the reader is led to the choice solution. If the conclusion is offered baldly and without alternatives, then anyone with another idea is able to champion it, putting the auditor on the defensive.

2. Choice of terms

It is important to give both problems and opportunities a name that can be remembered and agreed upon. Thus the auditor should avoid terminology which has become contentious within this particular organization, and find (or even invent) a word or words which provide a focus for action. If the organization has been fretting about 'lateral communication', then the auditor should address the problem and its solutions through some other vocabulary. The report will stand a better chance of implementation if it galvanizes people with a sense of opportunity than if it wallows in the gloom of identifying problems.

In putting forward the analysis, it is preferable to build on 'buzzwords' that people know – provided they are agreed upon and positively thought of. 'Communication climate' or 'corporate culture' are familiar to most people as a result of recent popular books and articles. What is more, these concepts are geared to the idea of an organization as a system of systems, rather than as a mechanism. They are based on the way people behave and seek to understand why people do what they do, rather than authoritarian structures which attempt to find the 'perfect organization' – which most people would probably instinctively distrust even if it could be achieved.

3. System-based approach

The data has highlighted details about who is talking to whom about what, why and through what channels, but all this information is secondary to the effectiveness of the organization, its competitive stance, its chance of improvement. These crucial issues are the product of all the minds which work together, responding not only to the immediate environment within the organization, but to the organization's place in society, in its sector, geographical location, market and role in the economy.

Such characteristics as questioning how people behave, willingness to share values, capacity to interact creatively are all related to communication. The auditor should be able to make an overall assessment of the organization, identifying its character, personality and the shared reality of its members. Sub-cultures or counter-cultures will probably be found which the auditor may want to see both encouraged (in the case of questioning how people behave) or discouraged (in the case of personality based feuding). The auditor should seek to give management a heightened self-awareness of their organization, on the basis of which they can develop and grow.

4. Sensitivity to corporate culture

A communication audit is not a measure of how happy people are, but nonetheless 'satisfaction' is an important aspect of communication. When people are not communicating well, they rarely say that they are satisfied. However, there are many ways in which people can communicate that are not productive of satisfaction for everyone, particularly definable minority groups, despite the fact that communication style is seldom seen as objectively good or bad by the participants.

Some organizations have a high degree of 'macho' in their culture, which can be observed in the language the members use; others are more 'gentle' in speech and culture. Neither extreme is right or wrong, although it is likely that if there is uneven expectation of what the organization's overall style is, then there will be unhappy, uncommunicative people. Some people communicate forthrightly in terms which to others might seem rude or offensive: others spend a great deal of effort on nurturing conduct in which people tend to wear their emotions more visibly. Communication in either case can be well or badly done, either through inappropriateness (being macho in a nurturing organizational culture) or through what is perceived as 'game playing' (which is frequently a matter of playing the wrong game for that particular place and time).

Analysis in these terms need not be threatening, particularly if it is related to such well-known organizational paradigms as the Hersey-Blanchard situational leadership format. (See: appendix, p. 188.) Indeed, clients are often pleased to identify themselves with different locations on these schema, after which it is possible to talk about 'appropriateness' rather than 'right and wrong ways of doing things'. An executive can understand that he or she needs to move towards participating rather than 'selling' a certain way of behaving because his or her personality is not at issue, but rather communication techniques which can be learned and implemented.

Organizations, like people, have lifecycles; and as it is inappropriate to expect a teenager to behave like a middle aged person, so it is pointless to ask a three year old organization to function like a 50 year old bureaucracy. The one will be more personality-led, the other more rule-dominated and impersonal. Each may be right for its particular situation. The formal, paper based communications of a government bureaucracy are not appropriate for a relatively small business entering the difficult and traumatic stage of expansion from a small proprietorship into company status, but nonetheless it is essential that such a business does not ignore the new level of complexity in its lifecycle by attempting to get by on the word-of-mouth, personal networks that characterize very small businesses.

The auditor should attempt to characterize the organization's historic status, as well as its individual characteristics, since it is reassuring to the organization to know that although it is moving into new experiences, nonetheless staff need not think that their situation is unique.

The auditor should not tell people what is wrong, unless he or she is going to give them a way to correct the situation. Simple though it is, this concept is at the heart of all consulting relationships, particularly communication audits. All too often at the report-writing stage the auditor slides into arrogant, threatening evaluation, as opposed to a consultative guide to improvement.

■ DEALING WITH PROBLEMS

The professional relationship between auditor and organization can be threatened or subverted by difficulties that can easily get out of control. If identified and coped with rationally, these problems can be turned to advantages; however if the auditor reacts either too aggressively or too passively, the situation can become disastrous.

There are four major types of discomfort during a communication audit. Recognizing them and taking appropriate action ensures that they do not become disasters. They are:

- misperceptions by employees
- misperceptions by the CEO
- intransigence
- personality clashes

Misperceptions by employees

Despite best attempts to follow advice about passport letters, face-to-face explanations and statements to groups about the purpose and nature of the audit process, the auditor may find that some people still feel threatened, and they may take action that can derail the entire audit. By failing to comply, spreading suspicions that the auditor is going to recommend dismissals or seeking 'hidden meanings' in the auditor's words or actions they can poison the atmosphere. The auditor must act forthrightly and fast. There are two related options.

(a) Meet with the person or persons concerned and attempt to 'start again' – that is, return to a neutral position. This can be done only by face-to-face interaction: written messages will be misinterpreted, and 'hidden' meanings will be read into them.

(b) If this simple approach either does not work, or the auditor judges that it might not work, a third party should be enlisted to act as neutral referee. Generally speaking, this should *not* be the CEO, who will feel obliged to 'back up' either the auditor or employee(s) in a situation where only a win-lose outcome is possible. If the auditor 'wins' due to an authoritative judgement from the CEO, control of the audit process will be lost and the auditor will no longer be seen as an objective evaluator. If he or she 'loses', then long before it is finished the audit will very probably end amid mutual recriminations, and quite possibly legal action as well.

Meeting unsatisfied employees
In most organizations there is a person known as a peacemaker who can be neutral and unbiased. The auditor needs to deal with facts, not emotions, but must also be sensitive towards emotions so that nobody feels afterwards that he or she has been co-opted by a trick or rationalized into compliance. The arbitrator must be someone who will take charge of the meeting or interview, letting emotional outbursts flare up and die away so that everyone can return to the source of the problem – which is usually a misunderstanding or misperception of what the audit is and does.

The auditor must be prepared to apologize, and to admit to mistakes in a way that will not undermine his or her authority. A statement such as, 'I'm really sorry that there has been this misunderstanding. We know now what caused it, and it won't happen again,' is acceptable to all parties. It is equally inappropriate for the auditor to demand abject admissions of fault from employees.

These 'peacemaking' sessions must not become dependent upon liking or trust. It is not necessary for everyone to like everyone – least of all for everyone to like the auditor: it is only essential that they respect his or her judgement. It is tempting to say or imply, 'Trust me . . .' but the reason for the meeting is that there has already been failure of both trust and communication, and so the temptation should be resisted.

Fisher and Ury's negotiation process is a good model for conducting the meeting. Be hard on facts, soft on personalities. Leave room for people to withdraw accusations. Allow for the occasional emotional reaction, and then return as quickly as possible to a factual statement of what has gone wrong and (more importantly) what can be done to correct the situation.

Misperceptions by the CEO

If difficulties are caused by misperceptions by the CEO, the problem is even more acute. The auditor may discover that he or she is being used by the CEO to find people to dismiss and should hold a meeting with the CEO immediately. Again, it is preferable that a neutral person be present, as the auditor will undoubtedly feel threatened, and the CEO may well perceive the situation as a challenge to his or her authority. Under these circumstances, emotions can get in the way of clear thinking, and what were intended as factual statements on both sides can be interpreted as having hostile implications.

Whether your problem is focused on individuals who the CEO is planning to dismiss, or whether it is a problem between different groups in the organization (management versus labour; senior management versus junior management; staff versus workers; etc.) the auditor must not allow him or herself to be used as a weapon in the war between 'us' and 'them'. A 'false solution' is deferment: the CEO, for example, may agree to defer all dismissals until after the audit. Not only is this fundamentally dishonest and unethical, it will undoubtedly affect the atmosphere in which the audit is conducted.

Meeting the CEO

At a meeting with the CEO, the auditor must return to basic principles, and make use of the original (written) description of what an audit is, and what it entails. Seek an agreement that provides a 'level playing field' in which the CEO's authority remains intact (in his or her mind), and the CEO's or the auditor's credibility is not compromised. Negotiate, do not dictate or be dictated to. Point out that the success of an audit can be predicated on the same factors as the success of everyday communication, and that by allowing the process to continue as it should, the problems with individuals or groups may well be solved.

As before, the auditor should not ask for trust or liking, but should generate confidence believing in his or her own methods. Look for ways of resolving what may be misperceptions by the CEO about his employee or employees. Admit that it is possible that your study may well turn up reasons for which people can legitimately be dismissed or demoted, but also point out that if this is the case, both due process and common sense point to the fact that this must have been going on before the audit began.

Intransigence

Very occasionally, an auditor encounters intransigence, that is, a person or people who do not respond to the foregoing attempts at peace-making or compromise. Should someone totally and deliberately refuse to cooperate, the best recourse is to establish him or her as a 'hostile witness' – that is, to make it clear that a reasonable approach has been attempted and found ineffective, and so the audit will no longer regard that person's contributions or comments valid.

If the intransigent person is the CEO, then this is an even more serious matter. Should all attempts at correcting the situation fail, the best course is to refer back to the letter of contract or the job description and complete the audit exactly to specifications and as speedily and accurately as possible. The auditor should ensure that the CEO is aware of the reasons for this.

Personality clashes

The term 'personality clash' is a convenient label for an inconvenient situation. It encourages people – the auditor included – to dismiss the whole matter as beyond solution. It is therefore both an admission of communication failure and a refusal to try to overcome it.

As has already been observed, it is not necessary to like someone to work with him or her: if communication were limited to likes and dislikes, it would not be possible to organize at all.

The suggestion that problems are the results of personality clashes is in itself a misperception of the audit process and of the auditor's role. The auditor must deal immediately with such misperceptions before they harden into intransigence.

■ THE CASE STUDY CONTINUES

29 Jan. Beginning to understand

I need some more information: facts. What's more, I know where to find them. I'll talk to the word processor operator with whom Shelley likes to work, and find out how the three custodians of the keyboards work together and with their in-house clients. Then I'll talk to the secretary in Sales.

My problem is that I don't know as much as I should about what King will accept. He's been away a lot, and he has left me alone. The interview was distinguished by the fact that he didn't pull rank or tell me condescendingly that I was wrong or any such defensive measure. But I still need to know whether I'll be heard if I zero in on concerns that are more than a little critical of him personally. Of course, I'll write it as neutrally as possible, but he'll not be human if he doesn't see that the cap fits him, not his subordinates when it comes to coordinating information and setting precedents for effective communication.

The mixture of informal and formal communication is fascinating: King knows that people are led by something other than simple fact and logic, and he certainly also knows that decisions are made by logic, or he wouldn't be CEO. What I have to do is somehow mix the two better, so that he is giving people the facts they need to deal with the changing environment. That's it. It's the change that's upsetting the organization: it has the resources to cope, but it's not accessing them because it's not fully conscious that it needs to. And then there are all the masking problems that have grown up like weeds – Accounting doing all the work, Sales and Marketing not talking, Ethel Walters overloaded and disliked, and so on.

I think I know now what I'm going to write.

Chapter 12
THE INTERIM REPORT

It is difficult to visualize an interim report until it is clear what constitutes a final report. Therefore, this chapter and the chapter on the final report which follows must be read in conjunction and the auditor will find it useful to bounce back and forth between them. The auditor must feel confident about those aspects of the report which will need advance checking with the representatives of the organization.

An advertisement for a major hotel chain featured the slogan 'No surprises'. This concept lies behind the interim report. The organization should not be shocked or surprised by the report – particularly not the CEO. The auditor does not wish to be alone and vulnerable when presenting the report, nor does the auditor wish to propose solutions which are out of the question, or worse still, make mistakes about the purpose and functioning of the organization.

■ THE INTERIM REPORT AS A DOUBLE INTERACT

The interim report is not an occasion for soft-pedalling or backing off from convictions. There is nothing unprofessional or compromising in the interim report process. Rather, it carries on the spirit of the double interact which should inform the philosophy and conduct of the communication audit.

The auditor can examine materials, knowledge and attitude before going into the interim report meeting by asking the traditional journalistic questions: Who? When? What? Where? Why? How?

Who?
The auditor should present the interim report, in person, to the CEO and, if appropriate, the person who has briefed the auditor should be present as well, though he or she should not be there for the whole time. There may be implications for him or her in what the auditor has suggested that need to be discussed with the CEO alone.

When?
The interim report should be presented to the CEO late enough in the

audit process that the auditor knows just about all he or she is going to know about the organization, but not so late that the conclusions are unalterable.

What?

The interim report is a draft of the final report. It is complete with respect to the introduction and description of the organization, includes the results of all the instruments, it is nearly complete with respect to analysis, but still may be tentative with respect to conclusions and recommendations. Data is accessible and clearly set out, but not yet in its final typed or graphic form.

Where?

The interim report session should be held in the room in which the auditor has been working, where all the documents are ready to hand. Failing this, a neutral space such as a conference room should be arranged. The auditor should disconnect the telephone, and/or arrange for someone to guard privacy for a few hours.

The CEO's office is *not* a good place to meet, even though he or she will quite possibly suggest it.

Why?

Once again, the auditor is negotiating a new reality, setting up the agreement necessary for constructive change.

How?

The presentation of the interim report to the CEO should be done in an informal working session. The auditor should present the report out loud, walking the CEO through it rather than having him or her take it home and study it, when he or she may become overly concerned about detail.

Especially if the auditor is working alone, it is a good idea to have a tape recording made of the entire meeting. Everyone will probably feel a little nervous and defensive, and under these circumstances it is easy to over-play individual problems on both sides. Only mature and disinterested evaluation afterwards will show the auditor how to overcome difficulties to everyone's satisfaction. (Of course, it should be made clear that the occasion is being taped, and the purpose should be explained.)

Guidelines for presenting the interim report

The auditor should bear the following 'rules' in mind when addressing the CEO.

- Neither crumple under discussion nor be too insistent.
- Take suggestions and objections, making sure that the nature of the problem is completely understood, rather than trying to have the auditor's own view prevail.
- Separate out those objections that are clearly major issues from nuances and shades of meaning in the expression of ideas.
- Remain calm.

The auditor called for this meeting as a final check that the analysis was valid and recommendations worthwhile. The auditor is attempting to implement positive change, and the CEO is the major agent of that change process. If he or she is not convinced by the report and recommendations, then little or nothing will come of them.

■ STRUCTURING THE MEETING

The auditor should structure the meeting as follows:

(a) Start with the introduction, and ensure that the description of the organization is acceptable. If the CEO does not recognize their organization in the description, they will not listen long or hard to much that follows. Take note of any corrections or amendments, and make sure they go into the final text. Do not rely on verbal explanations: if anyone has a problem with wording, chances are other people will as well.

(b) Distinguish between natural human reluctance to take bitter-tasting medicine and the CEO's superior knowledge of what he or she can accept. Usually, the sticking point is money, so have a mix of both expensive and inexpensive solutions to problems, and remember that the first agreement to make changes is probably the most important in creating a climate of adjustment and improvement. Accordingly, do not head up the list of recommendations with the most difficult, contentious and expensive matters.

(c) Negotiate, do not pontificate. For example, do not hesitate to qualify by saying, 'This recommendation can be implemented over the course of a couple of years if you wish,' but also do not be shy about saying 'This sequence of events is important in my opinion because. . .' A good way of prefacing your report (or any part of it) is by saying, 'If you can see a better way from your knowledge of the business . . .'

(d) Do not forget that this interim report is a vital part of the communication audit process, and thus an occasion for practising what you have been preaching about listening, the double interact and the accommodation of beliefs, hopes and habits in a new social reality shared by everyone, in which there are no sides.

■ A CHECKLIST FOR THE INTERIM REPORT

From the auditor:

- A clear draft copy of the introduction, analysis and tentative recommendations
- Accessible data
- A willingness to become involved in a double interact

From the organization:

- At least two to four hours of meeting time, free of interruptions
- Willingness to let the auditor tape (or otherwise record) the meeting
- Recognition of the meaning of the words *interim* and *draft*

Jointly arranged:

- A room with a large table, preferably arranged so that the auditor can sit *between* the representatives of the organization so that everyone confronts the issues, not each other
- Coffee for breaks when things get tense
- Wall-charts, diagrams, organizational charts, etc.

After the meeting debrief yourself with the tape recording and your notes. Then the next day, after a good night's sleep when you are able to approach the entire project with a fresh view, start revising. Do not approach your revision process with a defensive or grudging attitude.

■ THE CASE STUDY CONTINUES

31 Jan. After the interim report

Well, I knew it would be an important session, but I didn't expect it to go on so long. For about two hours, we moved our way in detail through the report with both Shelley and King asking questions about how, why, how much – and sometimes who – all of which I answered or, in the case of the who, professionally avoided. Then, when I thought that the whole thing was going to be an anticlimax, King smoothly got rid of Shelley and we really got to work.

I itemized the problems: the mess in Accounting, the isolation of Marketing, the over-work in Transportation, the time spent on the phone in Sales, the bottleneck in the CEO's office. He listened, and then amazed me by lecturing me about the draconian measures he would start in the morning. 'Right. We reorganize, we institute paper-flow contact. And if Worsley and Scanlon don't start interacting with Design, they'll be out of here. I'll call them all together tomorrow morning and tell them what's happening.'

I was aghast. I took a big breath to argue, and let it all out again. Instead, I made some fresh coffee. He poked around the room at bit, looking at my graphs and charts and muttering to himself. I gave him his coffee, and he looked at me as if for approval.

I told him that many CEOs who have to face changes in their organizations deny that there's anything wrong, and that he had just done the opposite. Then I asked him to bear with me while we looked at the whole picture before taking action. I talked about Regal's corporate climate and how much that is a product of this personal style. I showed him the mathematical, incontrovertible evidence of the sense of belonging among the majority of employees, their willingness to work with and for him. He interrupted a couple of times, worrying about the minority groups and asking why most people saw themselves as more interested in relationships than the firm. I pointed out that to know the sub-groups and their problems made it possible to do something about them, and that the fact that they can relate more personally is entirely in harmony with the way he talks with them.

Eventually, he admitted that Regal has evolved a style of operation that he could destroy by coming down hard on them, 'like Captain Bligh of the Bounty'. I thought about that Coast Guard painting, and asked him about it to change the mood a little. It was his ship, of course, as I should have guessed. Ernie Stokes and Joe Bailey served with him.

Then we got to the real problem, which is that he is going out on a limb with Regal, taking major risks, and he feels that he has to maintain a false front of confidence that he doesn't feel. (He didn't say this in so many words, but that was the message.)

I brought the whole thing down to practicalities and asked about money, trying to get some facts that would affect what equipment I recommend. It turns out Regal has good backing, plus personal investment by both King and his VPs who believe in Regal – and King. I heaved a sigh of relief, and then realized that King had just told me what he wanted to know.

We established what kinds of thing he could tell people, and I suggested how. We agreed that not telling creates speculation and destructive gossip. Finally, we decided to take things in easy stages, starting with getting the departments to talk together.

King seized on the notion of accessing information 'hidden' in the organization, recognizing that this would fit his personal style of operation. I had to dissuade him from wanting to organize this himself, but he saw that if the managers decide together, they'll follow what they regard as 'their' plans better than either King's or anything I could suggest.

I'm supposed to present my final report to the whole gang of managers, plus Shelley and Ethel Walters and the VPs. For a man who doesn't like meetings, he knows how to make someone else take charge of them! When we talked about the report, he asked me to spare everyone the foolishness of not having anyone on the telephone at lunchtime, and also to move the whole issue of maternity leave and other benefits into the past tense. I nodded at the first, but frowned at the second.

I'm going to make a softer report than at times over the past month I'd expected, but I think there's more chance of change happening after I've left if I put the implementaton squarely in their hands, with room for flexibility. King put it in nautical jargon, 'You give us the course and destination, and we'll worry about the steering and the speed.'

Chapter 13
THE FINAL REPORT DOCUMENT

When it is finished and presented to the organization, the report should be a complete record of the interaction which began the day the auditor set to work. The report is the auditor's product, the history of the audit, the lasting document on which the auditor's reputation will rest, so it is important that it reflects the professional standards applied to the audit itself.

Let us suppose that the auditor has opened the covers of the completed report and is turning the pages. The following chapter contains a sample final report document for our fictitious case study. Illustrations of these features can be found by referring to the appropriate part of Chapter 14.

■ THE LETTER OF TRANSMITTAL

The transmittal letter is bound into the report, at least into the master copy. It is a brief, formal note, which is the capstone of the entire project. It gives the date of completion and signals that the auditor has complied with the agreement into which he or she entered.

■ TITLE PAGE

Before the Contents and after the Letter of Transmittal, comes the Title Page. It is the auditor's choice how to set it out on the page, but the basic information is the name of the company, the auditor's name and the date.

■ CONTENTS PAGE

This page gives the readers a guide to what is in the report. It should therefore be clear, have numbered pages, and where relevant indicate subsections.

■ EXECUTIVE SUMMARY

This is the two or three pages that summarize the whole report. The auditor should write these *last*. The recommendations could be included in an uninterrupted list. It is important to be brief.

■ INTRODUCTION: THE ORGANIZATION

In these two or three pages the auditor 'plays back' or describes the organization to itself in such a way that all concerned will be able to agree that the auditor knows what the organization is and does.

METHODOLOGY

In one or two pages, describe the instruments and how they are used.

■ AUDIT DIARY

On this page, the auditor sets out what was done and where – the meetings, surveys, studies and reports. Essentially, this is a digest of the action plan, as modified by the realities encountered and simplified by what the organization needs to know.

■ THE RESULTS OF THE AUDIT PROCESS

In these 10-20 pages the auditor sets out the information gleaned from the use of the instruments. The following are useful guidelines:

- Take each instrument in turn, making as much use as possible of graphs, charts, diagrams and tabulated results.
- Explain or expand numbers so that they are *both* accurate *and* comprehensible. For example, say '77.5 per cent, or approximately three out of every four employees stated . . .', not just the percentage.
- Try not to put in *all* the numbers, particularly when the results of the survey questionnaire hold questions which are ambivalent or not particularly revealing.
- Do not conceal this information, however. Make reference to the appendix in which the complete data are presented – printouts, complete questionnaires, etc., and summarize in such a way that the important information comes clear.
- Give confidence levels and statistical justifications, and explain what they mean, but above all, don't mystify with numbers!

A useful technique for making information clear and unambiguous is to collapse five-fold preferences into three: for, neutral and against. This is entirely fair, since many people express their preferences cautiously. What is more, the auditor can show that he or she has collapsed data (*see* Table 13.1), and if asked, state why.

Question 1: Instructions received are usually clear			
Likert scale		%	Total %
1	Agree strongly	9.45	56.69
2		47.24	
3	Neutral	37.01	
4		3.15	3.94
5	Disagree strongly	0.79	
6	No response	2.36	

Collapsing and restating this data, more than half the population felt that instructions were usually clear, over one third were neutral, and a total of fewer than one in 24 disagreed.

Table 13.1 An example of collapsed data

■ CONCLUSIONS AND RECOMMENDATIONS

In the previous section the auditor gave the reader what has been found out; in these three to five pages it is made relevant. This is where the creative work is done. The auditor must be able to diagnose the ills and prescribe possible curative actions which are within the finance and skill capabilities of the organization. This analysis should be based on *what's right* in the organization, turning the strengths in such a way as to cure the weaknesses.

The recommendations (which should not come as a shock to anyone) should be brief, and prioritized. One approach is to separate recommendations into three:

(a) things which should be done now;
(b) things which may be done soon;
(c) things which can be addressed when time and money permit.

Another organizational principle is also three-fold:

(a) strengths;
(b) weaknesses;
(c) opportunities.

Whatever approach the auditor chooses, conclusions and recommendations should be set out so that they can be read independent of the rest of the report – because many people will go no further.

The auditor should always offer alternatives, of which the recommendation is the logical choice. For example, the auditor could have analyzed the organization and discovered that there are three serious information bottlenecks, corroborated by all of the instruments. The possibilities include dismissing the people who are the focus of the bottlenecks, giving them all assistants, giving them all computers, re-arranging the information flow, simplifying the information itself, and so on.

The analysis and subsequent recommendations should show that the auditor has considered all the possibilities and come to the best combination of actions in the recommendations. The auditor should tell the audience why such advice will solve the problem, show how that advice came from them through the interviews, studies, etc. This will give them a stake in the solution, rather than having the auditor do a magical act in which they are invited to believe with nothing to sustain them. They will have considered most of the alternatives – particularly the drastic ones – so the auditor should direct them through the alternatives to the recommendation on a path of logic.

If there are more than ten recommendations, the auditor should consider grouping them so that they end up in three sets of three. This is so that when the report is read and put aside, people can remember in general terms what is suggested. A hodge-podge of 36 excellent recommendations will be forgotten, or worse, recalled selectively.

■ APPENDIX

Here the auditor puts the raw data – the printout, the graphs and characters and numbers which cannot be presented in connected prose.

The auditor must be careful that the data does not infringe confidentiality, either by actual attribution ('Mary said'), or indirectly ('Two members of the marketing division complained that there was no pregnancy leave policy'), or numerically, when a statistical cell can be identified with the individuals it represents.

Copies of unfilled questionnaires, protocols for interviews, forms for network analysis, etc. should all be included. The information should be accessible, but the auditor need not expect that everyone will pore over every last syllable.

If the appendixes are either a) too thick or b) too confidential, one copy can be presented to the CEO, and the report circulated *without* appendixes.

■ THE CASE STUDY CONTINUES

4 Feb. Preparing the report
The wretched computer won't do double crosstabs, so I can't back up my point about the young women being unsure about maternity leave. I'll have to

make do with the anecdotal evidence of having talked with Carol, if anyone asks. I'm right, of course, but I'd love to have it in numbers.

Diagrams are going to be a bit of a problem. I've decided to go for neat, clear tabulations of the survey results rather than graphs that, although they give a picture, don't give numbers. The network analysis results should give people enough pictures to look at. King spent so much time working his way through all this at the interim report session that I'm not going to hide it away in an appendix.

I still have to prepare the boardroom and get some overheads made of select charts and graphs.

Chapter 14

PRESENTING THE WRITTEN REPORT

A COMMUNICATION AUDIT OF REGAL INSTRUMENTS

by

Pat Smith and Associates

February, 1987

Pat Smith & Associates

Mr. J. B. King
President, Regal Instruments

Dear Mr. King,
   Herewith find the final report of the
Communication Audit undertaken by me and my
associates for your company.

   Sincerely,

   Pat Smith

EXECUTIVE SUMMARY

Regal Instruments is a company in the process of transition into a new era
for the industry to which it has already made a significant contribution. It
has a strong organizational culture, based on values of loyalty, product
quality, timeliness, innovation and tradition, and a workforce that has some
of the best elements of both its origins in precision tools and its new
direction in electronic instruments. There is an information resource within
its members, that, if properly managed, can lead to success.

The communication structure of Regal Instruments was established when it
was a smaller, more homogeneous organization with only one product line.
Expansion has involved new facilities, products, designs, markets and an
incremental increase in staff. This has not been matched by corresponding
developments in its internal communication system. While the personal and
direct involvement of the Chief Executive Officer has ensured that he is not
remote from his staff, there has been a failure to actively promote
interaction among management personnel that would provide a team
approach to planning for the future, orchestrating beneficial change.

Nonetheless, there is an optimism and concern for improvement that can be
harnessed, provided information is shared appropriately among all levels of
the organization.

The recommendations of this communication audit address three
interrelated issues.

ii

A. *Optimizing existing strengths* in the informal communication structure.

B. *Correction of communication weaknesses* in ways that will harmonize with the existing organizational culture, specifically by improving interaction among the departments and their managers.

C. *Capitalizing on opportunities* by making the best use of electronic equipment to draw out and make use of information resources and skills available within the firm.

Implementation of the concepts in this report requires the creation of a Communication Group whose overall task is to manage:
- the development of better interaction among managers;
- the selection and implementation of appropriate electronic systems through joint planning and comprehensive training;
- the preservation and use of existing information resources.

Recommendations

Strengths and Weaknesses

1. That there should be increased communication among the department heads.

2. That components of the CEO's Secretary's job should be shared among people with appropriate communication training, freeing her to exercise her experienced judgement more efficiently.

3. That the discontinued practice of employee assessments should be reinstated, stressing the importance of individual career planning.

4. That the following matters be communicated both formally and informally:
  (i) changes to the benefits package;
 (ii) employee assessments as career planning opportunities;
(iii) group activities, jobs and achievements.

5. That Regal acquire a modern electronic telephone system.

6. That all departments acquire interlinked computing capacity.

7. That *The Regal Report* be expanded to take on new communication roles.

8. That an 'electronic signboard' system be installed in Production.

9. That a recorded telephone message system be installed in Sales.

Opportunities

10. That senior management endorse and actively promote the Mission Statement drawn up by the Audit Focus Group.

11. That a Communication Group be formed and made responsible for implementing communication and information improvements.

iii

12. That the Communication Group advise senior management in the reorganization of office space and department membership in order to enhance communication among related functions.

13. That the Communication Group plan and implement the electronic capture of select information resources within the company in the form of expert systems.

CONTENTS

INTRODUCTION

A Brief Description of Regal Instruments

Regal Instruments was founded in 1970 by J. B. King. Operating initially from a converted warehouse on Oak Street, Regal established a reputation for high-quality custom-manufactured tools for special purposes.

By 1977, Regal Instruments had captured a significant share of both the national and international markets for tools, instruments and other precision metalworking, but was still working from designs and prototypes supplied by researchers, designers and commercial clients. Recognizing the need for creative solutions to on-the-job problems in the construction industries, Regal Instruments established a Design section staffed by a group of people who shared both design ability and practical industry experience, and were capable of anticipating industrial needs.

Over the following five years, Regal expanded its international market, consolidating a reputation for product quality and reliable, timely delivery. In 1983, Regal launched its new line of electronic tools and instruments. Within a year, Regal's *Weldgage* was the industry standard gauge for measuring welds in a variety of difficult environments, thanks to having been accepted by underwriters as well as those actually working on constructing pipelines and pressure vessels in the oil and gas industries. Successive modifications and improvements have ensured that *Weldgage VI* is still a preferred measuring instrument in a highly competitive market.

The success of not only the *Weldgage* line, but also a variety of custom-designed tools and instruments, allowed Regal to expand into new quarters in Riverview Industrial Park, taking on a further 36 staff, many of them skilled in the assembly of electronic components. Since then, Regal has secured several longer-term contracts to supply custom instrumentation to large firms involved in frontier research in conjunction with universities on two continents.

From an operation that at its founding employed 15 people, Regal Instruments now has grown to a payroll of 132 full time personnel in seven sections: Production (82), Design (9), Accounting (10), Sales (7), Transportation (6), Marketing (3) and Maintenance (7), all located at the new offices and production space at Riverview. The complement includes the executive officers: President and Chief Executive Officer J. B. King, two Vice Presidents and four staff not specifically attached to a section (CEO's Secretary, two Receptionists, a typist and a Communication Officer).

To supply information to its external audiences, Regal publishes an annual report and generates a variety of product-specific proposals and descriptive materials, including manuals (which are translated into seven languages by the University's Modern Language Department). Regal has installed word

(1)

processing capability to handle the paper flow, and has added a communication officer in the past 18 months among whose tasks are to act as general editor to all written materials, maintain a bi-weekly newsletter, facilitate production reports and improve internal communication and morale.

Maintaining effective communication among 127 people performing different but interlinked functions is not a trivial matter. Recognizing the need to periodically assess internal communication, in January, 1987, Regal Instruments retained Pat Smith to conduct a communication audit that would assess the present state of the company's internal communications, and make recommendations for the future.

AUDIT DIARY

January
5   Pat Smith meets with Regal Instruments (Shelley Peters) for initial discussions
8   Letter of Agreement (see appendix) signed between Pat Smith and Regal Instruments
12   Shelley Peters provides conducted tour of Regal to Pat Smith
13   Action Plan approved
14   Focus Group approved
15   Survey approved, Focus Group meeting
16   Content Analysis material defined
19–23   Survey administered
20–22   Interviews
23   Technology Assessment Focus Group
26   Network Analysis day
30   Interim Report to J. B. King
February
6   Final Report presentation

METHODOLOGY

The methodology employed in this audit is to correlate the findings of five different approaches.

1. A survey yielding quantifiable, statistical data on employee perceptions, cross-tabulated against demographic data to provide an understanding of communication needs

(2)

2. A network analysis yielding conceptual diagrams of informal and formal communication flows

3. A content analysis of written materials yielding an understanding of both the content and style of formal communications

4. A focus group session with selected employees yielding a negotiated statement of corporate goals, as well as an up-to-date sample of employee perceptions and expectations

5. A series of interviews of key personnel yielding qualitative accounts of existing situations, opinions and perceived needs

6. A technological assessment yielding specific information on uses of and satisfactions with existing communication technology, as well as perceived needs

Each of these approaches can be regarded as a different feedback opportunity for the members of Regal Instruments to express their communication needs and preferences. By 'triangulating', that is, comparing the same issues as they appeared in each set of results, it is possible to provide objective corroboration of opportunities and problems independent of individual personalities. Empirical evidence authenticates more subjective accounts, which in turn enrich the numerical results with qualitative material.

RESULTS OF THE AUDIT PROCESS

1. Survey

Between the 19 and 22 January, 1987, 127 of the 132 members of Regal Instruments filled in survey forms, for a response rate of 97 per cent.

With very few exceptions which will be examined individually, all 24 of the questions were fully and clearly answered, yielding good data from which valid conclusions can be drawn. Statistical analysis revealed excellent significance in a confidence level of 95 per cent. Cross-tabulations between demographic and opinion questions revealed useful information about the communication needs of specific groups.

Annotated graphic data on each of the questions plus select cross-tabulations follow.

Graphic data

Note 1: m = mean; a * is placed beside the group closest to the mathematical mean.

Note 2: StD = Standard Deviation. The lower the StD figure, the tighter the concentration of cases around the mean.

(3)

Question 1: Instructions received are usually clear

1 Agree strongly	9.45%	}	56.69%
2	47.24%*	}	
3 Neutral	37.01%		
4	3.15%	}	3.91%
5 Disagree strongly	0.79%	}	
6 No response	2.36%	m 2.457	StD 0.915

Collapsing and restating this data, more than half the population felt that instructions were usually clear, over one third were neutral, and a total of fewer than one in 24 disagreed.

Question 2: Quantity of information received usually adequate

1 Agree strongly	3.15%	}	46.46%
2	43.31%	}	
3 Neutral	33.07%*		
4	15.75%	}	18.95%
5 Disagree strongly	3.15%	}	
6 No response	1.57%	m 2.772	StD 0.969

Collapsing and restating this data, slightly fewer than every second person felt that the quantity of information he or she received was adequate, one third were neutral, and one in six people disagreed.

Question 3: Information received usually arrives on time

1 Agree strongly	0.79%	}	14.08%
2	13.39%	}	
3 Neutral	57.48%*		
4	22.83%	}	25.19%
5 Disagree strongly	2.36%	}	
6 No response	3.15%	m 3.220	StD 0.845

Collapsing and restating this data, fewer than one in six people felt that information arrived in time to do their jobs, more than half were neutral, and one in four felt that the information did not arrive on time.

Question 4: Information received usually clearly expressed

1 Agree strongly	0.79%	}	37.00%
2	36.22%	}	
3 Neutral	48.82%*		
4	8.66%	}	10.23%
5 Disagree strongly	1.57%	}	
6 No response	3.94%	m 2.858	StD 0.940

Collapsing and restating this data, more than a third of the people felt that the information they receive is clearly expressed, nearly half the people were neutral, and one in ten felt that the style was inappropriate.

Question 5: Style of information is appropriate

1 Agree strongly	1.57%	
2	25.20%	26.77%
3 Neutral	31.50%	
4	10.24%*	
5 Disagree strongly	9.45%	19.69%
6 No response	22.05%	m 3.669 StD 1.533

Collapsing and restating this data, one in four people felt that the information they receive is conveyed in an appropriate style, one third are neutral, and nearly one in five felt that the style is inappropriate. More than one in five did not answer the question, leading to the speculations that they either did not find the question relevant, had no opinion, or did not understand the force of the question.

Question 6: Staff are able to provide information to others

1 Agree strongly	3.15%	
2	34.65%	37.80%
3 Neutral	25.20%	
4	2.36%	
5 Disagree strongly	10.24%	12.40%
6 No response	24.41%	m 3.551 StD 1.680

Collapsing this data, more than one third felt that they provided necessary information for others to do their jobs, one in four were neutral, and approximately one in eight felt that they did not provide information. The large number of non-responses (one in four) can be interpreted as an indication that one in four people does not perceive him or herself as passing information relevant to other's jobs.

Question 7: Staff are usually consulted about job matters

1 Agree strongly	0.00	
2	12.60%	12.60%
3 Neutral	26.77%	
4	17.32%*	
5 Disagree strongly	24.41%	41.73%
6 No response	18.90%	m 4.102 StD 1.332

(5)

Collapsing this data, fewer than one in eight people felt that they are consulted on job-related matters, slightly more than one in four were neutral, and two in five felt that they are not consulted. Nearly one in five did not indicate an opinion, leading to the speculation that they did not expect to be consulted.

Question 8: Staff are usually consulted about the company's future

1 Agree strongly	3.15%	6.30%	
2	3.15%		
3 Neutral	5.51%		
4	14.17%		
5 Disagree strongly	51.18%*	51.18%	
6 No response	22.83%	m 4.756	StD 1.153

Collapsing and restating this data, one in sixteen felt that they are consulted, one in twenty were neutral, and more than half of the people did not feel that they are consulted. Nearly a quarter of the people did not answer this question, leading to the speculation that they did not expect to be consulted.

Question 9: Channels used

Face-to-face, one-to-one	48.03%
Written	14.17%
Telephone	12.60%
Group meetings	12.60%
Other	10.24%
No response	2.36%

Interpreting this data, nearly half of the people use face-to-face, one-to-one as the most important channel of communication on the job. Written, telephone and group meetings are approximately equally represented.

Question 10: Channels preferred

Face-to-face, one-to-one	56.69%
Group meetings	18.90%
Written	13.39%
Telephone	3.94%
Other	2.36%

Interpreting this data and correlating it with Question 9, slightly more people prefer than get one-to-one communication, whereas almost twice the number of people who get group meetings want them. Written is preferred by more than those who receive it, and telephone is preferred by fewer people than who use it. Excepting the telephone, there is a strong preference for use of the three leading channels that is apparently not being satisfied in fact.

Question 11: Most information comes from superior

1 Agree strongly	11.02%	
2	51.97%	62.99%
3 Neutral	22.05%*	
4	7.09%	
5 Disagree strongly	3.15%	10.24%
6 No response	4.72%	m 2.535 StD 1.174

Collapsing and restating this data, nearly two thirds of the people got most of their job-related information from their superiors, only one in ten did not get information this way, while those who answered neutrally most probably had a mixture of sources for their information.

Question 12: Most information comes from co-workers

1 Agree strongly	3.15%	
2	13.39%	16.54%
3 Neutral	37.01%	
4	16.54%*	
5 Disagree strongly	14.17%	53.71%
6 No response	15.75%	m 3.724 StD 1.378

Collapsing and interpreting this data, approximately one in six people got their information from co-workers, while slightly more than half did not, and approximately one in three presumably got information from a mixture of sources. (This does not contradict the previous question.)

Question 13: Most information comes from subordinates

1 Agree strongly	3.15%	
2	4.72%	7.87%
3 Neutral	9.45%	
4	7.09%	
5 Disagree strongly	37.80%*	44.89%
6 No response	37.80%	m 4.850 StD 1.322

Interpreting this data, fewer than one in ten got information from people they view as their subordinates. The heavy response to items 4, 5 and 6

(7)

indicates that almost three quarters of the people did not get information from subordinates, and the no response classification indicates that one third felt the question irrelevant, presumably because they do not see themselves as having subordinates.

Question 14: Staff can trust senior management

1 Agree strongly	24.41%	
2	34.65%	} 59.06%
3 Neutral	21.26%	
4	0.79%	
5 Disagree strongly	6.30%	} 7.09%
6 No response	5.51%	m 2.323 StD 1.385

Collapsing and interpreting this data, it is clear that eight out of ten people trusted senior management, with more than two thirds emphatic about this trust.

Question 15: Trust among co-workers

1 Agree strongly	24.41%	
2	33.86%	} 58.27%
3 Neutral	33.86%	
4	3.94%	
5 Disagree strongly	0.79%	} 4.73%
6 No response	3.15%	m 2.323 StD 1.105

Collapsing and interpreting this data, nine out of ten people trusted their co-workers, more than half of them strongly.

Question 16: Satisfaction – hours

1 Agree strongly	2.36%	
2	23.62%	} 36.22%
3 Neutral	65.35%*	
4	6.30%	
5 Disagree strongly	0.79%	} 7.09%
6 No response	2.36%	m 2.748 StD 0.816

Collapsing and interpreting this data, more than nine out of ten people were satisfied or neutral about working hours. Further examination follows.

Question 17: Satisfaction - pay

1 Agree strongly	1.57%	} 25.19%	
2	23.62%		
3 Neutral	65.35%		
4	6.30%	} 7.09%	
5 Disagree strongly	0.79%		
6 No response	2.36%	m 2.882	StD 0.773

Collapsing and interpreting this data, more than nine out of ten people were satisfied or neutral about their pay.

Question 18: Satisfaction - benefits

1 Agree strongly	3.15%	} 26.77%	
2	23.62%		
3 Neutral	44.88%*		
4	18.90%	} 22.84%	
5 Disagree strongly	3.94%		
6 No response	5.51%	m 3.134	StD 1.098

Collapsing and interpreting this data, seven out of ten people were satisfied or neutral about benefits.

Question 19: Satisfaction - advancement

1 Agree strongly	0.79%	} 18.11%	
2	17.32%		
3 Neutral	33.07%		
4	33.07%*	} 41.73%	
5 Disagree strongly	8.66%		
6 No response	7.09%	m 3.528	StD 1.119

Collapsing and interpreting this data, approximately half the people were satisfied or neutral about opportunities for advancement.

Question 20: Challenged by job

1 Agree strongly	3.94%	} 24.41%	
2	20.47%		
3 Neutral	42.52%		
4	19.69%	} 24.41%	
5 Disagree strongly	4.72%		
6 No response	8.66%	m 3.268	StD 1.211

The bi-modal nature of this data demands further examination.

Question 21: Demographics - age

Over 60	1.57%		
50–59	20.47%		
40–49	42.52%		
30–39	36.22%*		
20–29	4.72%		
under 20	8.66%	m 3.992	StD 1.158

Question 22: Demographics - gender

Male	55.12%
Female	37.80%
No response	7.08%

Question 23: Demographics - time with company

More than 15 years	8.66%		
10–14 years	21.26%		
5–9 years	28.35%*		
1–4 years	28.35%		
Less than 1 year	9.45%		
No response	3.94%	m 3.205	StD 1.243

Question 24: Demographics - education

High school	66.93%
Diploma/certificate	18.11%
Bachelor	3.94%
Master	1.57%
Doctor	8.66%
No response	0.79%

Checking with the Regal personnel records reveals that only 2 people have doctoral degrees. Apparently, this question was used for light relief by some of the respondents. The distribution of high school and diploma/certificate responses agrees with the Regal records.

Cross-tabulation

In the following tables, p = probability, where any figure LESS than 0.05 indicates a significant probability to the correlation.

The percentages will not total 100, since non-responses have been deleted for the sake of clarity.

The numbers in brackets are actual numbers of people.

Questions 7 × 21: Consulted about job matters × age

	Older	Middle	Younger
Consulted	4.0% (5)	3.1% (4)	5.5% (7)
Neutral	3.1% (4)	5.5% (7)	15.8% (20)
Not consulted	2.4% (3)	14.1% (18)	22.0% (28)

$p = 0.0005$

There is a significant relationship between age and consultation about the job. The older a person is, the more likely he/she is to be consulted.

Questions 8 × 21: Consulted about company × age

	Older	Middle	Younger
Consulted	2.0% (3)	1.6% (2)	2.0% (3)
Neutral	0.0%	2.4% (3)	1.4% (3)
Not consulted	6.3% (8)	16.6% (21)	36.0% (47)

$p = 0.0000$

There is a significant relationship between age and being consulted about the company, even stronger than the foregoing cross-tabulation.

Questions 10 × 21: Preferred channel × age

	Older	Middle	Younger
Face-to-face	4.5% (7)	15.0% (19)	32.3% (41)
Group	0.8% (1)	1.6% (2)	13.1% (6)
Telephone	0.0%	0.8% (1)	3.1% (4)
Written	3.1% (4)	5.5% (7)	4.7% (6)

$p = 0.0000$

There is a significant relationship between age and channel preference. The younger a person is the more likely he/she is to prefer face-to-face and group situations.

Questions 10 × 22: Preferred channel × gender

	Male	Female
Face-to-face	36.4% (43)	21.2% (25)
Group	3.4% (4)	16.1% (19)
Telephone	3.4% (4)	0.8% (1)
Written	11.0% (13)	2.5% (3)

$p = 0.0003$

Gender preferences become clear in the above table, with women preferring groups, men telephone and written communications. It should be noted that there is substantial agreement about face-to-face communication.

(11)

Questions 16 × 21: Satisfaction with hours × age

	Older	Middle	Younger
Satisfied	7.1% (9)	4.7% (6)	20.4% (26)
Neutral	2.4% (3)	18.1% (23)	33.8% (43)
Not satisfied	0.0%	0.0%	2.4% (3)

p = 0.0000

There is a significant relationship between satisfaction with hours and age, the older a person is, the more likely he/she is to be satisfied. (There was no significance to the cross-tabulation of satisfaction with hours and gender.)

Questions 17 × 21: Satisfaction with pay × age

	Older	Middle	Younger
Satisfied	5.5% (7)	4.7% (6)	11.6% (16)
Neutral	2.4% (3)	18.1% (23)	41.8% (53)
Not satisfied	1.6% (2)	0.0%	2.4% (3)

p = 0.0000

There is a significant relationship between age and satisfaction with pay, the older a person is, the more likely he/she is to be satisfied. (There was no significance to the cross-tabulation of satisfaction with pay and gender.)

Questions 18 × 21: Satisfaction with benefits × age

	Older	Middle	Younger
Satisfied	7.9% (10)	7.9% (10)	11.0% (14)
Neutral	0.8% (1)	13.4% (17)	30.0% (38)
Not satisfied	0.8% (1)	1.6% (2)	15.0% (19)

p = 0.0000

There is a significant relationship between age and satisfaction with benefits, the older a person is, the more likely he/she is to be satisfied.

The large number of dissatisfied younger people prompted the following cross-tabulation.

Questions 19 × 22: Satisfaction with benefits × gender

	Male	Female
Satisfied	19.5% (23)	9.3% (11)
Neutral	33.9% (40)	10.2% (12)
Not satisfied	4.2% (5)	19.5% (23)

p = 0.0001

Males are much more satisfied than females. Taken with the foregoing table concerning age, it is likely that younger women are more likely to be the dissatisfied group.

Questions 19 × 21: Satisfaction – advancement × age

	Older	Middle	Younger
Satisfied	3.2% (4)	4.7% (6)	8.6% (11)
Neutral	3.9% (5)	3.1% (4)	23.6% (30)
Not satisfied	1.6% (2)	15.0% (19)	22.9% (29)

$p = 0.0000$

There is a significant relationship between satisfaction with advancement and age, the older a person is, the more likely he/she is to be satisfied. (There was no significance to cross-tabulating satisfaction with advancement and gender.)

Questions 20 × 21: Challenge × age – No significance

Questions 22 × 23: Time with company × gender

	Male	Female
More than 15 years	4.2% (5)	2.5% (3)
10–14 years	14.4% (17)	6.8% (8)
5–9 years	23.7% (28)	5.9% (7)
1–4 years	12.7% (15)	17.8% (21)
Less than 1 year	3.4% (4)	6.8% (8)

$p = 0.0101$

Men are more likely to have been with the firm longer.

2. Focus Group

Two focus groups were held during the audit process:
- (i) communication and the mission statement (this section of the audit report)
- (ii) assessment of communication technology (see page 25).

Communication and the mission statement

Eight Regal employees and staff representing every level of the organization formed the mission statement focus group, which met for three and one half hours on the seventh day of the audit process.

The declared objective of the session was to rewrite the mission statement of Regal Instruments by going through a process of negotiation and exchange that would describe the situation as it presently exists. From the interaction of perceptions at different levels and sections of the organization, it was possible to understand some of the differences of opinion that exist within Regal Instruments, and to make a first step towards the reconciliation of divergent views.

The formulation of a mission statement cannot be achieved in an afternoon, nor should it be drawn up by only eight people. However, the focus group was able to offer a draft statement that provides a basis for further work.

Mission statement

> Regal Instruments designs and manufactures specialized precision tools and instruments for the metal-working and equipment-operating aspects of the construction industry worldwide.

The foregoing statement resolves a number of conflicting views about the main focus of Regal Instruments, and was acceptable to all the participants. The group members were aware that Regal is in a process of change and development, thus the statement is clearly understood to be a definition for the time being, and in no way infringes on future plans.

During a warm-up exercise to clarify self-perceptions in the context of the organization, a consistent pattern emerged. The focus group cross-section of Regal employees and staff all felt that the organization as a whole was less concerned with human values than they were themselves. This tendency co-existed with a marked agreement among the participants that Regal has an appropriate concern for tasks, functions and internal organizational 'bureaucracy'.

While this exercise should not be considered to be evidence that Regal is a 'cold' or 'heartless' organization, it is a consensus statement of a need for a more human and personable environment.

The focus group consisted of:

> Mark Sangster, Vice President
> Lisa Fremden, Manager, Design
> Daniel Scanlon, Marketing
> Paul Frost, Sales
> Carol Manning, Receptionist
> Ernie Stokes, Supervisor, Production
> Bill Phipps, Production.

3. Interviews

Thirteen interviews provided the opportunity to enquire more fully into the roles, responsibilities and functions of different departments, in order to understand better how communication can take place in Regal Instruments.

The following protocol or checklist ensured consistency among the interviews.

Interview protocol

- Introduction: 'Rules of the game', confidentiality.
- Tell me your formal responsibilities.
- Are there other responsibilities? What are they?
- To whom do you report? How? Is this effective?
- With whom do you interact? Is this successful? Why? Why not?
- Do you need more information? What?
- Do you find that the information you get is accurate?
- How are decisions made in your section? In the organization?
- Is there a difference between various kinds of decision?
- Do you run into conflicts? What kinds? About what?
- How do you fit into the overall purpose of the organization?
- Have you any ideas you would like to see implemented?
- Are there any problems in getting your ideas heard and adopted?
- How does this organization 'talk' to itself? To others? How could this be improved?
- Can you think of something that I should have asked you?

Results of the interview process

The significant results of the interviews for communication purposes fell into three categories:

  (i) generic problems
  (ii) specific problems
  (iii) opportunities and advantages

(i) Generic problems
Interviewees felt that there was inadequate communication among departments. This emerged explicitly as analytical statements and through anecdotal information, and implicitly through expressed 'feelings' and 'concerns'.

The needs were in the main specific and task-focused. Information necessary to day-to-day work appears to be travelling effectively downwards through the organization, but lateral communication necessary to effective planning and anticipation of needs is not taking place. The isolation of the different departments is particularly apparent in the lack of exchange between Sales, Marketing and Design, where market information is lagging behind attempts to reach that market with desirable products. Administrative exchanges between Transportation and Accounting and the other departments are effective, although at times over-loaded.

It should be made clear that this is a problem of information not flowing at all, as opposed to inappropriate, confused or bad communication.

Upward communication is perceived as a problem by managers and employees alike. Information about anticipated problems is not reaching senior management, and although reaction to difficulties is prompt, there is a consensus that many of these could have been avoided if authority was

(15)

either vested lower within the organizational hierarchy (at the managerial level) or if communication could be swifter and more effective.

Again, it should be noted that there is an awareness that changes are likely to continue at an increased rate, and that senior management's concern has been directed towards policy and planning. However, there is a growing perception that senior management is becoming increasingly remote.

Related to these practical problems is the need for more information concerning the future of Regal Instruments. There is a high level of confidence in the solidity of the firm as a whole, but at the same time, there is a growing sense of anxiety about the effects of change on individuals and departments. This stress level is interpreted differently by different people: some welcome change, some are apprehensive. However, all exhibit a strong 'need to know', and the opinion was offered by several people at different levels that if facts were not forthcoming soon, hearsay would start to undermine confidence.

(ii) Specific problems
There are information overload problems at three locations in Regal Instruments.
   (a) In Transportation, which is operating at full capacity, frequently involving overtime.
   (b) In Accounting, which has inherited a number of non-accounting functions.
   (c) In the CEO's office, which must juggle day-to-day matters, 'organizational firefighting' and planning initiatives.

(iii) Opportunities and advantages
The interviews provided a window into Regal Instruments' organizational culture. At the close of two days of open-ended discussion, a pattern emerged in the dynamics that makes Regal Instruments a firm with a 'character' that is recognized by all its members, and that contributes in an important way to its position in the marketplace.

Regal has a strong sense of its values and reputation.

Product quality is regarded as a matter of trust and morality, rather than simply a technical issue of quality control within arbitrary parameters. Comments emerged during the interviews such as, 'People depend on us,' 'If our tools aren't reliable, we could have deaths on our conscience,' 'We make tools that people hang onto because they really work well.'

Regal has several 'company legends' arising from letters from satisfied customers. These are reportedly well-known among the staff and employees, and provide a strong incentive towards the maintenance of high standards.

Timeliness, or the importance of getting products to clients when they need them, is a highly respected value. This value permeates the organization, and can be seen in a willingness to complete jobs rather that letting them hang over to another day. This spirit communicates itself to newcomers in actions such as the way in which people leave the building each day: there is no wild rush out the door at 4:30, but rather people at all levels complete their tasks, even if it takes a few minutes more on occasion. Consensually, overtime is not requested until the job runs more than at least quarter of an hour beyond formal hours.

Innovativeness and tradition are at first glance contrary values, and indeed some of the friction within Regal can be traced to the clash between these two values. Since both are inherently positive motivating forces, and do not necessarily contradict each other, they can co-exist.

Innovativeness is a value particularly strongly held by those people who are working in new product lines developed in the past three years. Tradition is strongly valued by those people whose job focuses on products that have been produced by Regal for the past decade.

Personal loyalty is highly valued. This is focused on the CEO, whose regular visits throughout the firm are an essential part of the informal structure that provides cohesiveness and solidarity at Regal.

A number of legends permeate the organization that express these values informally, in anecdotal terms. These are powerful motivators, but it should be noticed that with the recent expansion of Regal's staff, the process of adopting norms of belief and conduct has become overloaded by numbers. The unoffical mentoring characteristic of past expansions has been over-extended in some areas, causing sub-cultures to spring up that are not in accord with the way that the dominant values are expressed. This is not to say that the values are not held or respected, only that there is a tendency among younger newcomers to regard the company legends and stories that express the values as outdated. (Often this is a matter of choice of words: a well-meant expression such as 'Old hands take the new person under their wing for a bit,' has been interpreted as patronizing.) This generates an abrasive atmosphere that neither group wants, but which is the product of lack of shared experience and/or language. Nonetheless, despite these difficulties, there is a rich opportunity offered by informal communication in Regal, and one which must not be overlooked.

Those interviewed were:

J. B. King, CEO	Mark Sangster, VP
Lisa Fremden, Manager, Design	Ben Wills, Manager, Accounting
C. Franks, Manager, Production	Michael Worsley, Manager, Sales
Daniel Scanlon, Manager, Marketing	Joe Bailey, Manager, Transportation
Carlo Santini, Production	Shelley Peters, Communications Officer
Michael Wiggins, Supervisor, Production	Mariella Comeau, Transportation
P. Shaughnessey, Manager, Maintenance	Ethel Walters, CEO's Secretary

4. Network analysis

A network analysis was conducted on January 26, during which each member of Regal Instruments was asked to keep track of communication events, whether spoken or written, in person, by telephone, in meetings (of more than 2 people) or in visits (one-on-one). A final question asked each person to rate the day's workload on a 1 to 5 scale between unusually slow to unusually busy. The results of that question indicated that 93% of the 123 responses (of 127 possibilities) rated the day 'average' (collapsing together 2, 3, and 4 on the 1 to 5 scale).

It should be noted in what follows that this analysis only claims to be 'typical' or 'representative' of communication activity in Regal Instruments, and should be used only to point to major presences or absences of communication, not to attempt to make predictions or evaluations precluded by the single-day, one-time nature of the data.

Having sounded a note of caution, there are strong indications from the network analysis that Regal Instruments should consider taking action to alter several tendencies. Analysis and recommendations follow in the next two sections.

The data that follows was compiled by making a master-chart of all the interactions recorded during network analysis day, and drawing the following 'communication maps'. The maps:

- examine the formal departments of Regal to see how they each communicate within their organizational framework;
- compare the formal lines of communication indicated by the Regal organization chart with actual inter-departmental communication;
- identify groups or 'cliques' characterized by the fact that the people in them are frequent intercommunicators.

Regal departments

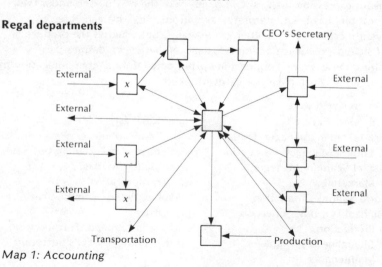

Map 1: Accounting

(18)

Accounting has a 'wheel' configuration, which is characterized by the supervisor (indicated by the box) in the middle. This arrangement is stable, leader dependent, slow to change and not conducive to groups solving complex problems.

Accounting has a number of links to non-supervisors of other departments which are explained by the need for discussion of specific projects at the level of sorting out details. External links outside Regal are similarly project-specific, those marked x concerned almost exclusively with word processing.

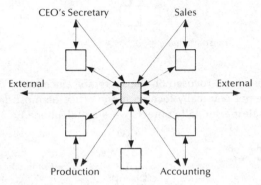

Map 2: Transportation

Transportation, like Accounting, is a wheel-shaped communication network, with some inter-department and external links on a project-specific basis.

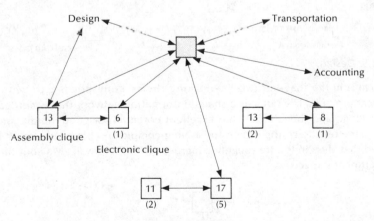

Map 3: Production

Production is a hierarchy, with six supervisors taking responsibility for the indicated numbers of people. Numbers in brackets indicate the people reporting direct contact with the department head (other than through their supervisor). See also analysis of cliques.

(19)

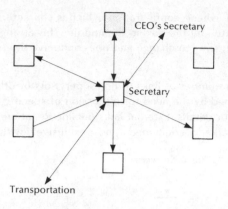

CEO's Secretary

Secretary

Transportation

Map 4: Sales

Sales is another wheel, focused on the secretary, since many of the
department are not physically located in the office on most days. (Excepting
one link by a salesperson, all contacts were by telephone.)

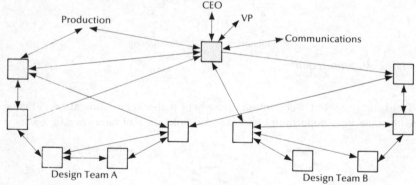

CEO

Production

VP

Communications

Design Team A

Design Team B

Map 5: Design

Design is in the shape of two interlocking circles, corresponding to two
current projects. The circle is a shared-information network that is not leader
dependent, and though slow, has excellent potential for good morale and is
the characteristic configuration for solving complex problems. It should be
noted that the circles are roughly congruent with the physical lay-out of the
department's space.

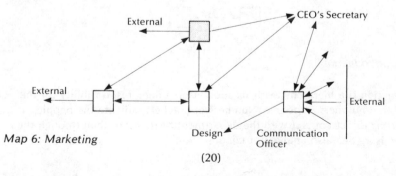

External

CEO's Secretary

External

External

Design

Communication
Officer

Map 6: Marketing

(20)

Marketing is divided into the four people designated to that department and the Communication Officer who is essentially 'housed' in Marketing.

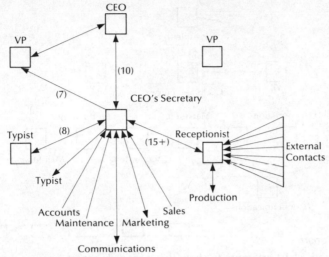

Map 7: CEO's office

The CEO's Office is by far the most active communication web in Regal Instruments. Numbers in brackets represent an attempt to clarify the number of times some communication took place (all of it face-to-face) although the people involved stated that they had to estimate, since they were too busy to note down every interaction.

The CEO's Office has within it a Y-fork, focusing on the Secretary, who must channel contacts between a number of sources and the CEO and VP.

Formal lines and communication links

The formal organizational chart appears in Regal Instruments' Annual Report as follows:

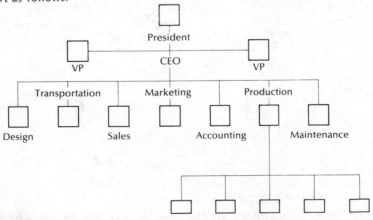

Organization chart

(21)

This is a graphic statement of a relatively 'flat' organization, with only one (larger) department having a lower management or supervisory level.

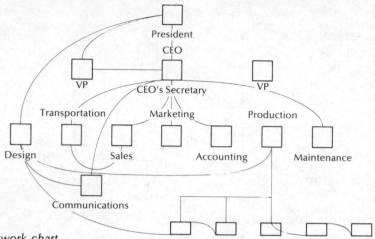

Network chart

The network chart attempts to show the informal, actual lines of communication on network analysis day. Only one such link (CEO's Secretary to Maintenance) was written. It is important to note how tightly tied the organization is, and how few isolated members there are. On the other hand, comparison to the formal chart shows that there are far more indirect contacts than might be expected.

Cliques

There are two significant cliques or sub-groups within Regal, both within Production. They have been identified as:
- (a) the electronic clique;
- (b) the assembly clique.

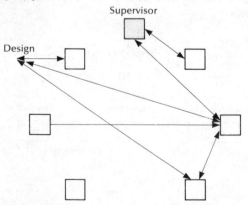

Production electronic clique

It should be noted that this loose clique includes Design through a triple linkage.

(22)

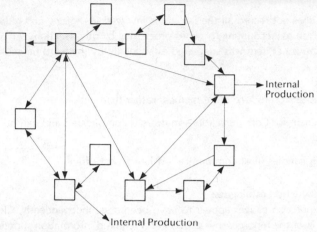

Internal Production

Production assembly clique

The Production Assembly clique is made up exclusively of women working on the assembly desks. It is tight-knit and virtually exclusive.

5. Content analysis

A content analysis of written messages in and out of Regal Instruments was conducted by a selective sample process. First a sample day was chosen at random and its written materials analyzed to generate categories of different kinds of message. Then a month-long period (November 15 to December 15) was surveyed, one week of which was examined in detail. The results are based on that carefully-studied week (November 3 to 10) and revealed the following paperflow in an average seven days at Regal Instruments.

Subject	No	Type	Source	Destination	Action
New gauge	1	10 page report	Design	CEO	approved
Gauges	1	5 page report	Marketing	CEO	none
Orders (s)	25	form	Sales	Production	filled
Orders (m)	4	form	Sales	Production	filled
Orders (l)	3	form + memo	Sales	Production	in process
Ship (out)	54	varies	T'p't	varies	completed
Ship (in)	11	varies	T'p't	varies	to Production
Invoices	54	form letter	Accounting	customers	recorded
Bills	32	varies	Accounting	creditors	paid
Payroll	127	cheques	Accounting	staff	paid
Catalogues	5,000	booklets	Marketing	varies	mail/pay
Pot-plants	1	1 page memo	Maintenance	CEO, Dept Heads	none
Newsletter	150	8 pages	Marketing/ Communication	Accounting	distribute
Ads	2	¼ page	Communication	CEO, Accounting	approved, inserted, paid
Plants	1	2 page memo	CEO	Dept heads	file
Orders	1	form + memo	CEO	Marketing	none
Release	1	draft letter	Communication	Design	
Money	83	letters	Communication	Accounting	mail/pay

(23)

Note
The table does not record all the iterations involved in drafting and redrafting material given to Accounting for word processing by other sections. An average of three iterations per item was suggested anecdotally by the word processing staff.

Comments
Memos appear to produce more memos, rather than action.

Approval chain for Communications matters is complicated and can be interrupted.

Accounting handles most communication like a post office.

Reports, newsletter, catalogues
The two reports on gauges appear to have been done independently. Close examination of the reports showed that each required information supplied by the other. The Design report was written in terse specifics; the Marketing analysis of Regal's and competing companies' offerings was focused on customer needs.

The catalogue mixes the two styles noted above. New products are described in technical terms only, older products have 'user-friendly' descriptions.

The newsletter is a well-presented, well-written tabloid-sized, single-fold, newspaper style production, entitled *The Regal Report*. It appears once a month. The editor is the Communication Officer, who writes more than 80 per cent of the stories. The other 20 per cent are either 'fillers', reprints from commercial magazines concerning the tools/instruments industry, letters to the editor, and a column written by a Regal employee whose identity is a jealously guarded secret. Five recent issues were examined in detail, yielding the following average contents:

Subject	*Column inches*	*Photo*
Social notes	30	2–3 per issue
Letters	0–15	
Sports	45	2–3 per issue
Anonymous columnist	10	
Filler	2–10	occasional
Industry notes	5–10	

A readership survey conducted by the Communication Officer in August (Report on file in CEO's office, dated September 10) indicates that most Regal employees (over 75 per cent) read the paper cover-to-cover, although a small number (10–15 per cent – possibly new employees) do not read it at all. The readership survey indicates that 37 per cent like the paper as it is, and do not want changes, 24 per cent would like 'more information about Regal', and 11 per cent would like more industrial news.

Other items examined in the content analysis that were not specific to the seven-day period included:
- — Regal employees manual
- — 25 Regal Instruments product brochures
- — 4 prototype descriptions
- — Brochure on Regal Instruments building

6. Technology assessment

A technology assessment focus group was convened on January 27, choosing people from Regal with a variety of experience and need for improved communication technology. The work of the Focus Group was broken down into distinct phases: brainstorming about what might be useful, and prioritizing that which might be possible.

During the first phase it became clear that there is a wide range of adaption to the use of electronic technology, ranging from those who prefer to ignore it to those who are highly adept in its use and eager to have the latest hard and software. Of the first group, none had any formal training in the use of computers, and (understandably) were therefore nervous of them. The second group were mainly younger or more recently educated in their field, or both.

During the second phase, the participants had no concrete ideas as to how much money could be spent on equipment and systems, and therefore were not able to apply the most decisive element in prioritizing.

Three scenarios were negotiated as the expensive, moderate and basic options:

1. *The expensive option*
   - — Messaging terminals for all department heads
   - — Micro computers in area networks for department members
   - — Extra CADCAM for Design

2. *The moderate option*
   - — Micro computers in area networks for select departments
   - — Extra CADCAM for Design

3. *The basic option*
   - — Micro computers for (select) departments
   - — Extra CADCAM for Design.

These three approaches recognize the importance of design having up-to-date equipment as being primary, but each approach also points to the need for inter-communication both within and among departments.

There was considerable discussion of the merits of training people to use computers, and the disadvantages of having a 'patchwork' of the computerized and non-computerized, or having varying protocols among a relatively small firm. There was general agreement on the need for adequate training in the use of any new systems, not only focused on the operators, but also on all potential users.

(25)

CONCLUSIONS AND RECOMMENDATIONS

The internal communication of Regal Instruments can be summed up in terms of:
A. Strengths
B. Weaknesses
C. Opportunities

A. Strengths

Regal Instruments has a strong corporate culture having values conducive to good communication. Regal's values, which are held by the majority of employees, are passed on orally by company legends.

Specifically, these values are:
- strong personal loyalty to the CEO;
- strong values of timeliness, product quality, innovativeness and tradition;
- strong informal communication network led by the CEO's practice of regular personal visits throughout the company;
- pleasant, potentially efficient work environment;
- experienced communication specialist on staff;
- some communication media already in place.

B. Weaknesses

Regal Instruments has grown from a small business style of operation to a departmental organization facing changes in product and market. The communication systems of the company have grown largely on an intuitive basis, more recently through deliberate design of the building and more specifically the installation of word processing equipment. The recent move and major additions of new staff have together strained both the formal and informal structures, and although the situation is not desperate, it requires attention to avoid serious problems.

Specifically these weaknesses are:
- inadequate communication among departments
- bottlenecking of information destined for the CEO
- isolation of definable groups
- inappropriate technology or use of technology

Inter-departmental communication

At present, the departments are held together by a loose informal network that is not focused on the heads of the departments. While on the one hand this informal structure is useful and efficient, it is not an appropriate channel for planning, analyzing and forming the cooperative strategies necessary to focus the entire organization on its goals. The network analysis results show a dramatic difference between the formal links suggested by the organizational chart, and the actual links shown in the network chart. Similarly, the survey shows a marked perception that people of whatever level are not consulted on either job matters about which they are competent to speak, let alone on plans for the company. Anecdotal information in interviews and focus groups points towards a felt need for more information exchange among the departments, specifically among Marketing, Sales, Design and Production. Accounting and Transportation have regular contacts with most departments on routine matters, but no policy or planning efforts at the level of the heads to improve these routine flows.

Recommendation 1
That there should be increased communication among the department heads.

Strategies
- Computerize, providing on-line information (desirable, but no face-to-face negotiation);
- Heads of departments meet daily (too frequent, too time-consuming);
- Circular memos (too slow, not in keeping with Regal's face-to-face style);
- Circulated 'daily report' (as above);
- Heads of departments meet weekly (recommended).

Meetings should be chaired by the CEO, reported by the CEO's secretary, who should prepare an agenda to which the heads can contribute. Frequency of meetings can be adjusted after not less than two months' trial period. Special meetings should deal with any issues that cannot be dealt with in an overall meeting of not more than an hour.

Bottlenecking

Information is not flowing between the CEO's office and the heads of departments. In part, this is addressed by the previous item and recommendations, but in addition to the lack of meetings, there is a serious weakness in the communication structure in that the CEO's Secretary functions in at least the following ways:
- gatekeeper who decides who should see the CEO;
- gatekeeper who decides who should answer incoming questions, complaints, etc., from outside Regal (and who answers most such questions based on her knowledge of the firm);
- unofficial senior secretary and focus of the informal information network;
- writer for the CEO (letters, reports);
- information source for CEO and VPs.

In addition, the CEO's Secretary is positioned in the office such that visitors automatically approach her desk first.

Recommendation 2
That components of the CEO's Secretary's job should be shared among people with appropriate communications training, freeing her to exercise her experienced judgement more efficiently.

(27)

Strategies
- Locate the Receptionist where the CEO's Secretary is now;
- Require the Receptionist to deal with the 80 per cent routine questions and referrals coming from telephone calls or visits;
- Require the Receptionist to turn over to the Communication Officer the 20 per cent unusual requests or questions, who in turn will either handle them or refer them to appropriate members of the company;
- Provide the CEO's Secretary's typist with word processing equipment.

Excluded groups

In the process of sudden growth during the past two years, larger numbers of new employees have joined Regal Instruments than ever before. The process of socializing that was one-to-one has not been replaced by any formal induction, and groups of people have consolidated who are outside the overall corporate culture. Misunderstandings have arisen between the 'new' groups who talk among themselves and the 'old' people, even though there may be no difference in chronological age.

Some of these misunderstandings are specific to a particular issue. This permits immediate action to address the heart of the matter. The importance of remedial efforts being successful and *seen to be* successful cannot be over-emphasized. The actual issues are relatively easily addressed; however, they are symptomatic of more serious problems.

The specific issues and groups are:
- The production assembly clique of younger women who are unaware of the recent review of maternity leave policy;
- The production electronic clique of younger men and women who value innovation above tradition and who seek advancement as a result of their special training;
- The Design Department, who espouse values similar to the Production electronic clique, but who are even more isolated from all but that clique and select members of Production;
- An ill-defined group of older members of the company who have from three to ten years before retirement, and who seek assurance about their continued usefulness to Regal Instruments.

Recommendation 3
That the discontinued practice of employee assessments be reinstated, stressing the importance of individual career planning.

Recommendation 4
That the following matters be communicated both formally and informally:
(i) changes to the benefits package;
(ii) employee assessments as career planning opportunities;
(iii) group activities, jobs, achievements.

Strategies
- Respond to the above agendas with information offered by: the CEO on his walk-arounds; The Regal Report; and updated pages of the Employees' Manual
- Hold 'product unveilings' in house
- Hold 'show and tell' sessions explaining both new and old skills and techniques
- Use the groups identified by the network analysis and the desire for more group information exchange discovered by the survey to deal directly with the sub-cultures within Regal, preferably with involvement from the CEO.

Information/communication technology

Regal lacks formal exchange among heads of departments, and it is to this need for face-to-face interaction that foregoing recommendations are addressed. There are in addition specific information needs that can be served electronically.

(a) Telephones: At present, Regal is served by a separate line to each of the different departments, plus a 10 year old switchboard at the main entrance. The discontent with telephones as a communication channel undoubtedly arises from this antiquated arrangement.

Recommendation 5
That Regal acquire a modern electronic telephone system.

Alternatives
- Install phone system with video (useful to noisy areas in Production, comparatively expensive);
- Install electronic phone system with features including call forwarding, conference calls, voice-messaging, computer-compatibility through modems (*recommended*);
- Install soundproofed booths in Production, signal by flashing lights instead of buzzers, integrated with electronic signboard.

(b) Computers: At present, Regal has in addition to CADCAM machines in Design and Production, four micro computers in Design and three word processors in Accounting.

Design and Production are making full and appropriate use of their equipment, but their output could be more efficient if their micro computers were linked together, allowing for better use of printing machines and inter-department communication.

The three computers presently located in Accounting are used primarily for word processing letters, reports and routine forms. This represents an inappropriate use of machines and trained personnel, since information is being created in other departments, passed to Accounting for word processing, passed back for checking, passed back for final corrections, before it can be sent to its destination.

(29)

Accounting makes virtually no use of the calculating (strictly, the *accounting*) capabilities of the machines within its control, because so much of the machine time is taken up with repetitive typing chores better done by the primary authors of this material.

Transportation is using manual methods to interface with electronic machinery used by shippers, customers and transportation companies. The efficiency of this department is such that it has managed to stay ahead of its competitors, but it represents a misuse of time and energy not to employ the resources of computers for accessing and processing information as well as speeding up and increasing the accuracy of repetitive work.

The primary needs of the different functional units are:
- Accounting: calculation, records;
- Transportation: access to data banks, filling forms, records;
- Production: scheduling, communication, inventory;
- Design: graphics, calculations;
- Sales: communication, records;
- Marketing: access to data banks, graphics, word processing;
- CEO's office: word processing, communication;
- Communication: word processing, publishing, graphics.

In addition to filling these primary needs, a computer network within Regal could improve internal communication, simplify scheduling and integrate activity.

Recommendation 6
That all departments acquire interlinked computing capacity.

Alternatives
— Sell the existing micro computers and standardize work to word processors (ignores the graphics potential of the micro computers library of existing programs and files);
— Sell the word processors and standardize work to suit the micro computers, (ignores mathematical potential of word processors library of existing programs and files);
— Sell both sets of machines and install a mainframe computer (ignores training, experience, files, programs, expertise);
— Acquire two or more word processors and two or more micro computers, basing the choice on the preferences of the departments. Create two interlinked networks, using the new file-translation technology that allows 'translation' from one system to the other. (This machine is approximately the size of a personal computer, and can be attached to a word processor as a peripheral.) (*Recommended*).

(c) Print:

Recommendation 7
That *The Regal Report* be expanded to take on new communication roles.

Alternatives
- Continue as at present (expressed needs for information are ignored);
- Establish a new source of information (ignores the support for the existing paper);
- Allow *The Regal Report* to provide information on changes within Regal, offer functional information useful to its readership, promote improved communication and morale. (*Recommended.*)
- See recommendations 4, and 9–12

(d) Other media: Other opportunities exist for appropriate information-giving and exchange in addition to those mentioned. Production has problems in getting messages to members on the job.

Recommendation 8
Purchase an 'electronic signboard' system for Production.

Alternatives
- Continue as at present (noise makes universal communication in Production a serious problem);
- Install video screens (costly, inappropriate for simple graphics and words);
- Ensure that input to the screen can come from both the department head and the telephone receptionist (*Recommended*).

Recommendation 9
That a recorded telephone message system be installed in Sales.

Strategy
At present, a great deal of the Secretary's day is spent making or receiving contact by telephone with Sales personnel in the field in order to give them similar information. A recorded message system on a dedicated line would allow Sales personnel to check with head office at their convenience on a daily basis, receive the day's information, and discover whether they needed to speak individually to the secretary or department head.

C. Opportunities

As has been indicated indirectly in the foregoing, Regal Instruments has a great number of communication opportunities for which it is ideally prepared, given some of the corrections and additions already noted. Most importantly, Regal has good morale, and can easily improve it still more. The sense of individual and group confidence that can be enhanced by good communication will lead to exploitation of the very considerable human resources of the firm. The following recommendations address ways of continuing to enhance this process.

Regal Instruments has professionals with developed skills in communication and information-handling, some acquired through formal training, others through varied experience. Drawing together these people into a Communication Group will ensure that communication and information remain a high priority, and that implementation of this report is accomplished smoothly.

Recommendation 10
That Senior Management endorse and actively promote the Mission Statement drawn up by the Audit Focus Group (*see:* page 13 of report).

Alternatives
- Continue as at present (differences of opinion exist as to the main goals of Regal Instruments);
- Await a major strategic planning session when the future becomes more clear (proposed statement can be changed at a later date);
- Actively promote the mission statement through all internal media as a means of focusing overall goals and evaluating specific activities (*Recommended*).

Recommendation 11
That a Communication Group be formed, responsible for implementing communication and information improvements.

Strategy
The Communication Group should be based in Marketing-Communication, and be given authority to:
- choose hard and software in consultation with its primary (operator) and secondary (supervisor) users;
- plan and promote computer training appropriate to different levels;
- plan and promote awarness of Regal's mission (recommendation 10);
- plan and implement physical and conceptual changes to the communication structure, as necessary (recommendation 12);
- implement expert systems (recommendation 13).

Alternatives
- The Communication Group be based in the CEO's office (the office is overloaded with planning responsibilities already);
- The Communication Group be based in Accounting (the department should not take on further non-accounting tasks);
- The Group should include the Communication Officer, the head of Accounting and the CEO's Secretary (*Recommended*).

Recommendation 12
That the Communication Group advise senior management in reorganizing office space and departmental membership to enhance communication among related functions.

Strategies
The opportunities conferred by Regal's new building can be more fully exploited. At present, some floors are over-crowded, others sparsely populated. More

importantly to communication and information, closely-related departments are on separate floors. Accordingly the Communication Group should:
— relocate separate word processing terminals (present situation overloads Accounting, impoverishes other departments);
— bring Accounting and Transportation to the same floor (change should involve economies of time and messaging);
— move Design to lower floor (closer to Production, room to expand).

Recommendation 13
That the Communication Group implement the electronic capture of select information resources within the company in the form of expert systems.

Strategy
Expert systems catch and preserve information, experience and skills in such a way that the knowledge is available to others. In addition to primary tasks such as calculations, graphics, communication, data bank access, word processing, etc., there are advantages conferred on the company as a whole by this use of computers. In Regal Instruments there are valuable resources that contribute to the company's excellence, but are only tapped occasionally or by people who know about certain individuals' special skills and abilities.

The Communication Group should acquire appropriate programming capability, prioritize a work schedule and work out appropriate remuneration for the people who will make their abilities available. Specifically, the Group should consider:
— Ernie Stokes – metalworking knowledge and skill;
— Ben Wills, Ethel Walters – company history, 'contacts';
— Joe Bailey – international shipping and forwarding.

APPENDIX: THE QUESTIONNAIRE

Instructions

In the following questions, please CIRCLE the number which indicates your preference. For example:

1. The instructions I receive about what to do are usually clear.

Agree strongly				Disagree strongly
1	(2)	3	4	5

After each question there is space for your comments. If there is not room, continue your comments on the back of the page.

We start with the information you give and get on the job

1. The instructions I receive about what to do are usually clear.

  Agree strongly   Disagree strongly
   1   2   3   4   5

2. The quantity of information I receive is usually adequate for me to do my job properly.

  Agree strongly   Disagree strongly
   1   2   3   4   5

3. The information I receive usually arrives in time for me to do my job.

  Agree strongly   Disagree strongly
   1   2   3   4   5

4. The information I receive is usually clearly expressed.

  Agree strongly   Disagree strongly
   1   2   3   4   5

5. The style in which information is conveyed to me is appropriate.

  Agree strongly   Disagree strongly
   1   2   3   4   5

6. I can usually provide the necessary information for others to do their jobs.

  Agree strongly   Disagree strongly
   1   2   3   4   5

7. I am usually consulted on subjects about which I have information and expertise.

  Agree strongly   Disagree strongly
   1   2   3   4   5

8. I am usually consulted about plans for the future of my part of the company.

  Agree strongly   Disagree strongly
   1   2   3   4   5

Now let us look at what channels you use

In the following questions, *write in your evaluation of the order,*
where 1 = most, and 5 = least.

9. The channels of communication I usually use on the job are:

Channel	Order of importance
Face-to-face, one-to-one	☐
Telephone	☐
Written	☐
Group meetings	☐
Other (please specify)	☐

10. The channels of communication I prefer on the job are:

Channel	Order of preference
Face-to-face, one-to-one	☐
Telephone	☐
Written	☐
Group meetings	☐
Other (please specify)	☐

In the following questions, please *circle* the number which indicates your preference.

11. Most of the job-related information I get comes to me from my immediate superior.

Agree strongly			Disagree strongly	
1	2	3	4	5

12. Most of the job-related information I get comes to me from my co-workers.

Agree strongly			Disagree strongly	
1	2	3	4	5

13. Most of the job-related information I get comes to me from people who report to me.

Agree strongly			Disagree strongly	
1	2	3	4	5

Please write any other sources of job-related information here. Use the back of the sheet if there is not enough room.

Now let us look at some general questions

14. Generally speaking, I trust senior management.

Agree strongly				Disagree strongly
1	2	3	4	5

15. Generally speaking, I trust my co-workers.

Agree strongly				Disagree strongly
1	2	3	4	5

16. I am satisfied with the hours I work.

Agree strongly				Disagree strongly
1	2	3	4	5

17. I am satisfied with the pay I get.

Agree strongly				Disagree strongly
1	2	3	4	5

18. I am satisfied with the benefits package (holidays, sick pay, accident insurance, etc.).

Agree strongly				Disagree strongly
1	2	3	4	5

19. I am satisfied with my opportunities for advancement.

Agree strongly				Disagree strongly
1	2	3	4	5

20. I am challenged by my job.

Agree strongly				Disagree strongly
1	2	3	4	5

Now some general statistical questions about yourself

In the following questions, please circle the number *beside* the group to which you belong. Remember, you will not be personally identified in any way with or by this information.

(36)

21. Age

   1 Over 60
   2 50–59
   3 40–49
   4 30–39
   5 20–29
   6 Under 20

23. Time with company

   1 More than 15 years
   2 10–14 years
   3 5–9 years
   4 1–4 years
   5 Less than 1 year

24. Education

   1 High school
   2 College diploma
   3 Batchelor's degree
   4 Master's degree
   5 Doctorate

22. Gender

   1 Male
   2 Female

Thank you for your help. Please seal your questionnaire in the attached envelope and return it to one of the collection boxes.

■ THE CASE STUDY CONTINUES

It's over. I presented my report to Regal Instruments. King, both VPs, all the managers, and even the six supervisors from Production (who had to share a copy – even with four extras above the ten requested), Shelley and Ethel Walters. Only Maintenance was missing. When I asked why, Ethel told me that Patrick Shaughnessey had officially left Regal to start his own maintenance business, and his first client was – Regal Instruments!

The presentation went better than I had hoped, and a great deal easier than I had feared. I led them through the Executive Summary, expanding specifically on the strengths and weaknesses with excerpts from the results. They were fascinated by the network diagrams, and asked intelligent questions about the survey.

I led them up to the recommendations gently, prefacing them with the concept that implementation was Regal's business, their business, and that now they had to make it work. King nodded.

Scanlon looked very tense, and Worsley frowned until I got to the recommendation about a special 'phone line for Sales, when he cheered up. When Scanlon heard he was to be part of the Communication Group, I couldn't gauge his reaction. Then there were some trifling questions about the figures, a query from a Production supervisor who was clearly unsettled that I'd found two cliques in his department.

(37)

King stood up and thanked me formally, endorsed the report, noted that there was flexibility but a clear direction overall, and we all broke off for coffee and conversation. I detected a strong feeling of relief that it was all over, and I'm sure I wasn't just projecting my own feelings. Every one of the managers had had something to worry about, and they all spoke to me. Everyone was civil, except C. Franks of Production. He informed me that he didn't know why it took a month's work and all that paper to give Regal a blinding glimpse of the obvious, that he could have done in half an hour, and free. For the first time, I realized that he alone would see no benefits in the plan, because he's been working virtually on his own, making deals with Lisa Fremden that make him look good. Lisa, on the other hand, was almost effusive: 'You were so logical: I am amazed!' When the room cleared out a bit, Sangster came over to me and whispered that he had kept the firm's insurance company working overtime for three days to get the new contract that added maternity leave and special retirement benefits for long-term employees.

Shelley was pleased. I think she had hoped for more – her own department and an office on the CEO's floor, for instance – but she saw sense in the plan for participation, and she'll have her hands full to make the committee work. She had the advantage of having seen the draft so she had been watching the audience as I spoke and was also optimistic about the future.

Finally, I said a personal goodbye to King. 'We're not all going to live happily ever after now you've gone', he said. I agreed that this was a reasonable attitude to take, considering the negotiation and discussion that would have to follow. 'I never liked big meetings, and you've got me into a lot of them, I can see that clearly.' I suggested that it was not up to him to lead, chair, moderate or control them, only to be there and guide the people, as he had done during my presentation. He nodded slowly. 'Thank you', he said, 'I'll try that.'

I gathered up my papers and my own copy of the report, and headed out the door. In the downstairs lobby was Carol Manning. She gave me an envelope. Inside was my final cheque from Regal Instruments, duly signed by J. B. King.

PART FOUR

The Aftermath

Chapter 15
AFTER THE AUDIT, WHAT NEXT?

■ THE AUDITOR'S SELF-EVALUATION

Once the audit report has been completed and presented, there is still one more activity before the project is closed. The auditor should invite an assessment of the audit from the CEO. Approximately a week is a reasonable time to leave between the final report and the assessment.

The CEO's assessment provides the material for the auditor's own self-assessment. The fact that the auditor can be self-critical and accept the criticisms of others will increase the likelihood that he or she is offered further auditing projects. The auditor should not simply ask for reactions: it is better to provide the CEO with a form that will jog his or her memory and avoid replies that are focused exclusively on one good (or bad) aspect of the audit that sticks in his or her mind. A suitable format for this questionnaire appears below.

COMMUNICATION AUDIT ASSESSMENT

Please answer the following questions frankly. Your responses will be kept confidential unless you give specific permission for them to be quoted. Use the back of the form if there is not enough space for your comments.

A. The Conduct of the audit

1. Did you find Pat Smith well prepared for the task of auditing your organization?

2. Was Pat Smith professional in all dealings with you and your staff?

3. Did Pat Smith explain to you clearly the nature and purposes of the audit?

4. Did Pat Smith live up to commitments such as timeliness, confidentiality and efficiency?

5. Was the audit accurate with respect to an appreciation of what your organization is and does?

6. On the scale below, please assess the usefulness of the audit to you and your organization.

Very useful		Somewhat useful		Not useful
1	2	3	4	5

7. Will you implement the recommendations?

All of them		Some of them		None of them
1	2	3	4	5

8. How well was the audit presented to you and your staff? Did you find it clear, the points well taken, the analysis competent?

Very clear		Some cloudiness		Obscure
1	2	3	4	5

9. Did you find that the report balanced underlying theory and effective practice?

Good balance		Overly theoretical		Overly practical
1	2	3	4	5

The Concept of a communication audit

10. Would you consider another audit?

    Yes   No

If 'no', please indicate why not.

11. If you replied 'yes' to the foregoing question, would you consider Pat Smith as the auditor?

    Yes   No

If 'not', please indicate why not.

12. What would you like more or less of in any subsequent audit?

Your replies will be held in confidence unless you explicitly approve otherwise.

I approve the use of any of the above comments.

Yes   No

(Signature) _____

I approve the use of comments only if I am notified in advance as to which comments and to whom they are being referred.

Yes   No

(Signature) _____

I would be prepared to act as a referee to Pat Smith on the subject of communication audits.

Yes   No

(Signature) _____

(Position and Company) _____

■ THE ORGANIZATION'S EVALUATION OF THE AUDIT PROCESS

There are two possibilities for implementing the recommendations of a communication audit.

- The organization implements the recommendations
- An external consultant is employed to facilitate the implementation phase.

The first and more desirable alternative, is that the process started by an auditor should be continued to its logical conclusion by the organization itself. The participative process of the audit should create a willingness among all the organization's members to take part in ideas suggested by the recommendations, and it should no longer be necessary to rely solely on the auditor's view. Indeed, it is not even possible. The auditor's role as a person who is in the organization but not of it concludes with the final report. If he or she returns to the organization, it is in a fresh role: perhaps as consultant to a specific project, perhaps as a contractor supplying some particular item or skill from the repertoire of a communication professional, perhaps as an employee returning to regular duties after concluding the audit. In any

event, he or she will be in and of the organization, not at a professional distance.

The second alternative, wherein the organization brings in someone
to facilitate the implementation of the audit's recommendations, is entirely appropriate if the recommendations (or some part of them) can
be given project status, with a clear objective, work schedule and
conclusion. It is not defensible if the organization's senior management
merely wants someone to enforce and take responsibility for the recommendations by coercive means. Not only is this not in the spirit of the
audit process, but it also prejudices the possibility of using the audit as
a benchmark for other audits at a later date (in the manner of the
annual financial audit that has become a regular feature of business
and corporate life).

External projects arising from an audit

Some projects will flow naturally from the recommendations of a
communication audit. Introducing new technology, modifying the roles
and communication responsibilities of staff members, improving the
paper and verbal flows of the organization are all natural subjects for
projects that have specific goals and objectives that the audit has defined, and against which implementation can be measured.

There are also a number of external public relations project areas
that an organization might turn to as a result of an audit. These could
include:

- a general audit of external communications;
- assessment of interaction with specific publics (a specialized audit of
  communication with government, industry, community or other
  'affiliated' organizations);
- readership analysis of a company magazine or newsletter with a
  view to finding out how to reach the needs of the target public;
- redesign of marketing tools such as catalogues and brochures, based
  on a survey of target public;
- inauguration or extension of corporate events such as plant tours,
  open house days, product previews, etc;
- enhanced participation in marketing events such as trade shows.

The advantage conferred by holding a communication audit *before*
moving to these external matters, is that the organization is more likely
to know its communication strengths and weaknesses, to speak with
one voice and to be able to mobilize all its members in a coordinated
public relations scheme. Since nothing destroys effective public relations so quickly as the perception that they have been used purely to

smooth over difficulties, it is essential that internal communication excellence precede attempts to persuade external publics. A communication audit is therefore the first and best logical step towards enhanced advertizing and promotional efforts.

Internal projects arising from an audit

Frequently, a communication audit is the beginning of a continuing project in staff development. Unlike putting in new machinery or making adjustments to the reporting structure, staff development has no end-point at which one can say that the process is complete. Accordingly, its contributions to an organization are difficult to assess. This difficulty in evaluation causes many companies to regard the personnel function as strictly an administrative matter. However, organizations that have had a long-term concern for the lives of their employees are usually adamant about the benefits to all concerned – both to the individuals and to the company. These advantages are not limited to such generalities as 'improved leadership', 'loyalty' and 'good morale', but can be objectively demonstrated over time in pragmatic economic terms. Among the measurable benefits of human resources development are:

- decreased absenteeism and staff turnover rates;
- increased productivity;
- working 'smarter, not harder', resulting in all employees constantly looking for ways to improve products and processes;
- a more participative and less authoritarian style of operation, resulting in executives having more time for 'creative management' that seeks out challenges and opportunities rather than being obsessed with discipline and control;
- integration of the research and development function throughout the organization, as employees refine products, services and processes;
- better applicants for new positions and jobs;
- improved public relations as a result of all employees seeing themselves as ambassadors for the organization.

Human resource development can include:

- career planning within the organization;
- the preservation and extension of special skills and abilities built up over the years among employees through apprenticeships and the creation of expert systems;
- formal educational and training opportunities that are cost and/or time-shared with the organization;

- industry, professional, or sector-sponsored training, which may include seminars, conventions and industrial or professional association membership.

It also has a 'familial' aspect that can feature:

- day-care facilities in the workplace;
- intelligent and fair-minded employment of married couples;
- opportunities for second and third generation participation in the organization;
- discovery of skills and abilities among minorities not previously employed by the organization, including ethnic minorities and the handicapped.

All these human concerns are intrinsically worthwhile and ethically excellent. They also contribute to the community in which the organization lives and works and encourage a better social and educational environment. They are also investments in everyone's future in both economic and general terms.

Expert systems projects

A communication audit often discovers 'hidden' knowledge and expertise that can be among an organization's most valued resources. Whether by traditional means such as apprenticeship systems or with new technologies such as computer based 'expert systems' this information and skill can be maintained and developed within the organization.

Any such project must have the cooperation of those involved. A fair remuneration for the data-banking of individual expertise is essential. Even though the legal ramifications concerning the 'ownership' of skills and experience-gathered information vary from place to place, it is possible to arrive at mutually satisfying agreements that protect the individuals and the organizations concerned. Ethics and fairness decree that any creation of expert systems by employees should be remunerated generously. If that is not enough, organizational self-preservation is a strong motivator to ensure that employees do not merely take their skills and knowledge to competitors.

Familial organizations

Societal changes to traditions of family life over the past generation have meant that people are looking to their lives at work for satisfactions that used to be found in the home. Women are encouraged to have careers, married partners no longer assume that the man's job is their primary economic consideration, and small families of one or two children mean that women no longer must choose between marriage and career. The pressures to provide familial services within the workplace have never been stronger.

Astute organizations are aware that any extra expenses incurred by such services are more than offset by the benefits of having loyal, committed employees. In-the-workplace or industry-financed day care services attract young, highly-motivated staff, and make it more likely that they will not bounce from job to job.

Similarly, more and more people are reaching retirement age with a reasonable expectation of having twenty or more active years ahead of them. Companies and organizations that maintain a continuing relationship with their retired employees find that there are measurable benefits from doing more than awarding a 'gold watch and hearty handshake' at retirement. Company and organizational clubs have generated business resources that include new product and service ideas, family employment from generation to generation and excellent community and public relations.

Such long-term planning starts with day-to-day communication on the job, and is strengthened by consultative approaches to such matters as benefit packages.

Regular communication audits improve organizations

An important result of a communication audit is the planning of the next audit. Using the same techniques on subsequent audits allows for year-over-year assessments that report on improvements and monitor long-term projects.

No organization is static. The life-cycle of an organization mirrors that of nature if it is left alone to grow and develop without conscious control. While this can foster maturity of judgement and the amassing of valuable experience, it can also lead to blind traditionalism and consequent loss of competitiveness. The organizational equivalent of hardening of the arteries is inflexibility of internal communication flow. Ignored or glossed over, communication becomes one-way, stultified and unresponsive. Under these conditions, the organization goes into decline.

A vital benefit of repeated communication auditing is the uncovering of age differences that can easily be overlooked because of the simple fact that everyone grows older at the same rate. By examining the opinions of younger members of the organization, it is possible to maintain the best qualities from the past while capturing the enthusiasm and willingness to experiment that are characteristic of youth. Regular audits ensure that 'new blood' has the opportunity to enter the organization and make its contribution felt through communication that is open, effective and responsive to changes in the larger social environment.

■ AUDITS MAKE GOOD SENSE

Communication audits are no panacea. However, if they are responsibly contracted by executives who are open to constructive criticism, and conducted by auditors who are up to date in their profession and sensitive to both individual and corporate needs, then not only will the organization talk sense, it will respond sensibly to the many pressures and challenges of its business environment.

■ THE CASE STUDY CONCLUDES

King's answers to my questionnaire came in the mail today. He was generous, but critical as well. He's right that there should have been more detail on the interviews, but I don't know how. He would have kept the material confidential, but since it was passed out to all of his managers, I know that any more details would have been ascribed to the people concerned, and that wouldn't have been good. He wanted more detail in the content analysis, but I rather think he really expected me to read everything instead of taking a representative sample. I doubt that I'd have found very much more, even if the time available had made it possible to try.

He says he will implement most of the recommendations, but unfortunately, he doesn't tell which ones he won't. I doubt he can or will go back on his commitment to having the managers meet and recommend to him on the composition of their departments, and that has to be good news, no matter how much or how little gets done. He wrote a note on the back saying that Shelley is very pleased with her new responsibilities, so that's one weight off my mind. I'd been thinking that I should have given more detail to what she should be doing, but I held back for fear of getting into actual tasks such as brochures and annual reports.

Loose ends. King didn't pick up on the fact that I'd done little or nothing about Maintenance. The circumstances of Shaughnessey's change of status worked out fine, but I could have been unlucky.

Speaking of luck, or at least good fortune, I'm glad that Franks didn't declare war on me. He's the only one whose life may be less easy as a result of my audit, and he's certainly not going to be as well placed in the power structure as before. Come to think of it, that may not be so. First of all, he has a nose for power vacuums, and is willing to step into them. And he got what he needed from me: improvements to his work-space.

Then there are all the little things I'd have liked to change: the plant jungle upstairs that hides the senior executives, the way women have only first names while men get at least their surnames, if not a 'mister', the blatant equation of height in the building with height in the pecking-order. That at least should be mitigated by re-organization of departments.

Indirect news as a result of King's reply was that the letter was typed by 'CM'. I guessed it was Carol, and when I phoned, I made sure by asking for King's secretary. It was. And I was asked if I wanted to speak to Ms Manning, or to Mr King's Executive Secretary, Ms Waters. It looks as if Ethel has finally got her due.

I'll see if she's happy with her promotion on Monday. The last paragraph of King's letter asked me to come and see him about another contract, this one to assess and make recommendations about external communications!

Appendix

MAKING SENSE OF ORGANIZATIONS

Organizational communication is a relatively new discipline, even though organizations have been a fact of human life for thousands of years, and have been commented upon by a great number of thinkers prior to the last two generations. Military geniuses from Julius Caesar to Montgomery have stressed the importance of clear orders, good information and open lines of communication. However, it is only in the present century that there has been a deliberate attempt to understand how people communicate on the job, what motivates them, and how an organization can best make use of its human resources. What follows is a brief examination of:

1. Messages
2. Motivation
3. Leadership
4. Organizations
5. Systems

1. Messages

A generation ago, it seemed clear that messages are the units of communication. Scholars reasoned that if we understand how messages are passed, then we can optimize communication, particularly in organizations. In 1949, Shannon and Weaver proposed a 'mathematical model' of communication that was in its time a valuable contribution to understanding the technology of the day, particularly the telegraph or the military use of the radio (*see*: Fig. 1).

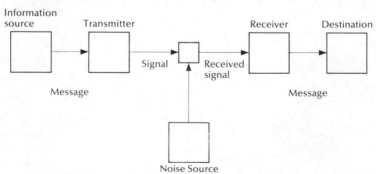

Figure 1 Shannon and Weaver's linear model of communication

The diagram offers a concept of how data is encoded, transmitted, circumvents or is distorted by noise, is received, and decoded. It is an adequate way of examining the technology of data transfer, but it totally avoids the human factors, the most important of which is that data does not become information until it is put into use by a human being.

Since Shannon and Weaver, we have come to understand both individuals and society much better. We recognize that a message can be misunderstood, misinterpreted or ignored. We are aware of linguistic, cultural, societal and individual differences, and no longer think of effective communication as a process of brainwashing everyone into using a limited set of words in exactly the same way.

Nonetheless, Shannon and Weaver's classic SMCR (Sender, Message, Code, Receiver) paradigm is still very apparent in the way many organizations function, particularly at times of stress when people feel that they need to get 'back to basics'. Communication auditors will recognize that the SMCR theory stands behind remarks such as, 'I sent a perfectly clear memo, and if they can't read, they shouldn't be working here.' Implicit in statements of this kind is the idea that messages are units of thought that can be shot like bullets from one person to another, killing opposition by taking possession of the other person's will.

A modern society with its complex organizations requires more sophisticated models of how communication works. We need to take into consideration not only the physical realities of jobs or tasks, but also the psychological realities of the people involved in the communication; and also the social contexts in which they are involved. This is what the convergence model of communication offers (see: Fig. 2). Convergence theory points to the way that communication can enhance (or degrade) the working of an organization in the process of deliberate change.

The diagram indicates that successful communication involves common perceptions, interpretations and beliefs. The outcome is mutual agreement and effective joint action that are the expressions of those same internal states. We know that people who disagree rarely work well together, and that if they are coerced into doing someone else's will they will seldom do the best job of which they are capable. Convergence theory shows us that if we achieve mutual understanding through communication, we are assured of coordinated action towards shared goals.

Unlike the mechanical SMCR model, convergence theory acknowledges that we are self-aware beings who not only communicate, but also know that we are doing so. All of us are on occasion critics of

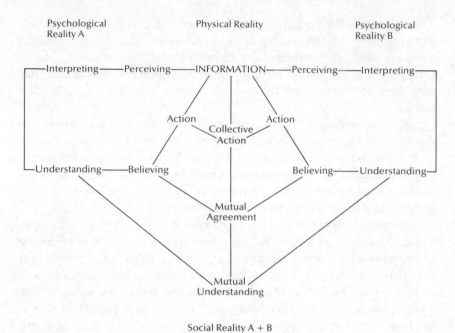

Figure 2 Kincaid's convergence model of communication

communication as well as communicators, evaluators as well as partici-
pators. We draw conclusions about executives and their motives, and
on these (sometimes inaccurate) convictions erect our understanding of
what an organization is, does and is planning to do. This is why a
communications audit examines not only what is said (the messages)
but also what the people in the organization think, feel and believe.

A simple expression of the convergence theory in a business context
was offered by Charles Redding, who called the process, 'The double
interact' (see: Fig. 3). An effective exchange follows the pattern, 'I talk;
you listen and then reply; I consider your reply and reply in turn, you
listen and confirm.'

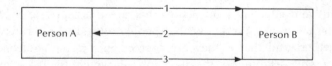

Figure 3 Redding's double interact

At first glance, this looks like the SMCR diagram again, with the
addition of a pair of feedback loops, and so it is. However, the *context*
is different in that Redding, like Rogers and Kincaid, is talking about

the exchange between two *people*, who are mutually aware in ways that cannot be duplicated by *machines*. It is on this awareness of emotions, perceptions, beliefs and opinions that an effective audit is based, because these are the sources of motivation that communication both addresses and expresses.

2. Motivation

In 1954, Abraham Maslow enunciated his 'Hierarchy of Needs'. This schema has influenced organizational communication theory ever since. While his approach was intuitive rather than empirical, it was founded on a great deal of scientific research, and it remains a classic approach to understanding why people work and how they communicate in the context of their work.

The five steps in Maslow's hierarchy are:

1. Need for self-actualization and autonomous self-respect
2. Need for respect and esteem from peers
3. Need for a sense of belonging, companionship and love
4. Need for safety and security
5. Need for food and shelter.

Maslow's hierarchy offers a framework for assessing the motivational level at which people are functioning, and it allow us to focus attention on how people are communicating about those needs.

Maslow employed a simple but effective method of evaluating communication that he called 'grumble analysis'. Realizing that 'man is a wanting animal', Maslow listened to the people who expressed to him what they wanted, and noticed that their grumbles were about the level of need at which they found themselves. He saw that people grumble because they want, and what they want is generally the next step up the hierarchy. A hungry man will rarely be concerned with qualitative ethical problems involved in achieving self-realization, because his need is to know where his next meal is coming from. Secure, well-fed people, on the other hand, will grumble about lack of respect, esteem or self-development.

Accordingly, the astute communication analyst attends to what people say they want not merely to establish a wish-list, but in order to find out at what level of motivation they are functioning. This leads to an understanding of how people may be further motivated.

Maslow's hierarchy helps us understand why a person who is making a substantial salary is often not motivated by a raise in pay – even when he or she takes it. If he or she is seeking personal rewards that are conferred by the esteem of peers or an internal sense of achievement, it is the *quality* of work, not its remuneration in terms of money that is important.

3. Leadership

For many years, leadership research concentrated on the idea that there was something called 'charisma' that leaders have as a gift, and that leadership consisted in getting people to abandon their own impulses and perform the leader's orders. However, in recent years, leadership has been studied in terms of the interaction between leaders and followers, and the group purpose expressed by the Chinese saying, 'Of a truly great leader, the people say, "We did it ourselves." This approach makes leadership a learnable, transferrable skill based on knowledge and understanding rather than on some mysterious 'talent'.

Hersey and Blanchard offered what they called 'situational leadership', or leadership styles appropriate to different situations. They reasoned that if the source of a leader's power lies in the consent of his or her followers, it is necessary to have operational criteria to allow a leader to assess his or her followers, in order to adopt an appropriate leadership style.

Hersey and Blanchard's analysis of followers (*see*: Fig. 4) is through assessment of task maturity, or ability to do the job. (Because it refers to a person's capacity to perform this task on this occasion, the term should not be confused with chronological maturity.) People can be:

Unwilling and unable	M1
Willing but unable	M2
Able but unwilling	M3
Able and willing	M4

People who are unwilling and unable (M1) require a leadership style that is styled to be high task and low relationship; that is, it focuses on what to do, when, and how to do it, and does not become involved in the interpersonal relationships that could 'muddy the water' of effective and appropriate communication for this situation. Hersey and Blanchard characterize this style of leadership as 'telling', since this is the most appropriate conduct on the part of the leader.

Telling is the imperative mode of leadership: it roughly corresponds to the lowest of Maslow's hierarchy of needs.

Selling is the leadership style appropriate to people who are willing but unable (M2). Selling is the persuasive, manipulative style. It is in the declarative mode, based on the logic, 'You all want to make a lot of money, and this is the way to do it.' A team of people whose interactive mode is selling are at about the mid-point of Maslow's

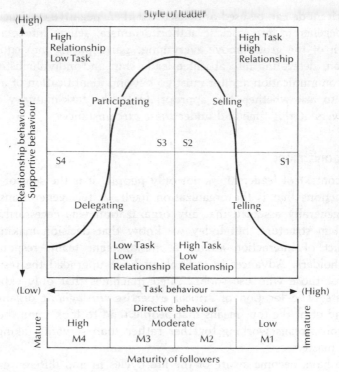

Figure 4 Hersey and Blanchard's situational leadership

hierarchy, and are concerned with a sense of belonging and companionship.

Participating is the leadership style appropriate to cooperation among people who are able but unwilling (M3), where guidance is required from a leader who does not need to insist on his or her authority or superiority. It is the conditional mode, expressed in statements such as, 'If we talk it over, we can decide what needs to be done.' Mutual esteem and respect are the needs in Maslow's hierarchy that are fulfilled by this mode of interaction.

Delegating is the style in which the leader becomes helper and facilitator to people who are both able and willing (M4). It is the subjunctive, impersonal mode and, in Maslow's terms, an invitation to self-actualization.

It must be noted that the four leadership styles are descriptive, not evaluative. While it may be that you or I might prefer to work in a participative or delegating leader-follower model, it is not our preferences that matter, but rather the task at hand and the task-maturity of the followers.

Each mode can be used or abused. At their negative extremes, telling can degenerate into fascistic authoritarianism, selling into placing the benefit of the group above everything, participating into endless discussion, delegating into absentee leadership and individualistic chaos. The communication auditor must go beyond identification of a leader's style to ask whether it is appropriate to the task-maturity of *these* followers at *this* time and under *these* circumstances.

4. Organizations

The context of leadership is not only people, it is the sum of all their interactions that is the organization itself. A few generations ago, it was generally assumed that any organization was necessarily hierarchical in structure, but today we know that decision making is the product of interaction among a management team, responsible to stockholders. Advances in technology have upgraded the responsibilities of those who use sophisticated machines that only experts can operate. The location of critical expertise *throughout* organizations, instead of at the top, means that people tend to look upon themselves as professionals working together rather than servants taking orders from masters.

We have become aware of the life cycles in and differences among organizations. From the simply structured small business to the complex and bureaucratic corporate giants of the business world, the art of management has created a variety of special functions including accountants, marketing experts, public relations people, research and development specialists, sales people, and production managers. Each of these areas of expertise must be coordinated into a smoothly-functioning whole, and moreover, operate within a changeable economic environment.

A communication auditor must be aware not only of the end purpose of the organization, but also of its specific individuality. Recently, the terms 'communications climate' or 'corporate culture' have been used to describe the character of organizations, since each one responds to its environment differently as a result of the blend of individuals who make up its personnel. There is no perfect communications model that can be held up as the ideal. However, there are norms that time and research have shown to be effective, as well as recognized procedures that are generally adopted by astute managers. One such norm is management by objectives. Simply stated, MBO is the objective statement of missions, goals, objectives, tasks and responsibilities, so that it is possible to understand what each person is to do, and why he or she is doing it, from the CEO to the most junior position in the organization. Clearly, since any such statement is in words and numbers, it must be communicated and understood in order to be effective. The identification and clarification of any such systematic approach to working and communicating together is critical to the success of a communication audit.

5. Systems

The significant difference between nineteenth and twentieth century thinking is our awareness of systems as opposed to simple causes and effects. Systems thinking is not difficult to understand, even though the outcome of systems research may well use complicated mathematics and sophisticated techniques of analysis.

Imagine a collection of coloured balls of various sizes and shapes – say approximately 100 – connected by rubber bands of varying thicknesses. Let each ball have one or more rubber bands connecting it to one or more other balls, and ensure that there are not simple generalizations that can be made, such as the large balls having large numbers or thicknesses or lengths of elastic. Now assemble this three-dimensional model so that there are a variety of tensions, distances and clusterings of balls, and so that no matter what ball is touched, all balls move perceptibly. The model is of a human organization, and the links are communication.

Step back and give one of the balls a whack. We can see immediate connections to the rest of the structure – the connections of this organization to its integral parts and to the external world.

The model represents an interdependent system of the kind with which we habitually deal intuitively rather than analytically. When we do this by simplifications such as, 'Let's just deal with the big red balls', any such reduction of the system into linear cause and effect necessarily ignores (or reduces to 'side effects') what happens to all the elements we leave out of our calculation. We have taken a three-dimensional, interactive situation and conceptually reduced it to simple, usually linear cause-and-effect sequences that do not offer a sufficiently powerful understanding to deal with the complexities of reality.

Until the advent of the computer and its capacity to perform many complicated mathematical operations virtually instantly, we either had to work from intuitions and hunches, or to simplify to grosser, more obvious linear connections. Today, the computer allows us to consider more factors, richer contexts and more complex systems, and to understand them in terms of a high level of probability that itself can be measured and assessed. Instead of absolute predictions that frequently are wrong or at least misleading, we have assessments of likelihood.

Because we know the risks and do not wager the future on one supposedly absolute truth, we achieve better decisions. Paradoxically, it is from qualified reliability that we can achieve more confidence about our predictions and decisions.

This is the context of a modern communication audit. It uses survey techniques that confer both objectivity and precision; it incorporates theoretical formulations that have stood up to practical testing. Finally and most importantly, it recognizes the uniqueness of each organization, and the individual dignity of every person.

Select Bibliography

Bernstein, David, *Company Image and Reality: A Critique of Corporate Communications*, Holt, Rinehart & Winston, London, 1984

Block, Peter, *Flawless Consulting*, University Associates, Burlington, Ontario, 1981

Booth, Anthony, *Communications Audits: A UK Survey*, University of Leicester, 1986

Cantor, Bill, *Experts in Action: Inside Public Relations*, ed. Chester Burger, Longman Inc., New York, 1984

de Bono, Edward, *Lateral Thinking for Management*, McGraw Hill, London, 1971

Emanuel, Myron, 'Auditing Communication Practices' in *Inside Organizational Communication*, ed. Carol Reuss and Donn Silvas, Longman, New York, 1981

Fisher, Roger, and William Ury, *Getting to Yes*, Penguin, London, 1983

Goldhaber, Gerald M., and D. Rogers, *Auditing Organizational Communication Systems: The ICA Communication Audit*, Kendall-Hunt, Dubuque, Iowa, 1982

Haywood, Roger, *All about PR*, McGraw Hill, London, 1984

Hersey, Paul and Kenneth H. Blanchard, *Management of Organizational Behavior*, 2nd Edition, Prentice Hall, Englewood Cliffs, NJ, 1972

Hofstede, Geert, *Culture's Consequences: International Differences in Work-Related Values*, Sage, Beverly Hills, CA, 1984

Jackson, Peter C., *Corporate Communication for Managers*, Pitman, London, 1987

Krippendorff, Klaus, *Content Analysis*, Sage, Beverly Hills, CA, 1980

Pfeffer, Jeffrey, *Organizations and Organization Theory*, Harper and Row, Plymouth, 1982

Redding, Charles W., *The Corporate Manager's Guide to Better Communication*, Scott, Foresman & Co., Glenview, Ill, 1984

Rogers, Everett M., and D. Lawrence Kincaid, *Communications Networks*, The Free Press, Macmillan, New York, 1981

Skibbens, Gerald J., *Organizational Evolution: A Program for Managing Radical Change*, Intersystems Publications, Seaside, CA, 1981

INDEX

action plan 25-7
age differences 181
anonymity 43, 45, 47 64
apprenticeships 179, 180
appropriateness 61
audit diary 127, 136
auditor 14
  self-evaluation 175
audit process 14
  organization's evaluation 177-81
  results 137-59
  selection 8-12
  setting up 13-18

benefits of communication audit 6, 8, 11, 111
'bimodal' response 54
bottlenecks 57, 105, 160, 161
brainstorming 39, 93, 104, 107, 159
brief 13-14

CADCAM 99, 100, 159, 163
career planning 162, 179
case study
  first contact 18
  walk around 27-9
  action plan 31
  focus group 40-2
  survey approval 55
  survey results 55-6
  network analysis 68
  interviews 77
  content analysis preliminary 87
  technology focus group 99-100
  beginning to understand 118-19
  after the interim report 123
  preparing the report 129-30
  presentation of report 171-2
  conclusion 182-3
checklists 16, 123
check-points 17
Chief Executive Officer (CEO) 4, 8
  approval of audit 45
  assessment of audit 175-7
  interview with auditor 22, 30-1, 117

misperceptions 117
  office 155, 161
  receipt of interim report 121-2
  receipt of report 104
clarity 45, 86
cliques, 64, 152, 156-7, 162, 171
code sheet 50
collapsed data 128, 138-43
committees 10
communication chain 65
communication channels 4, 48, 95-6, 140
communication circle 65
communication climate 5, 97, 113, 190
Communication Group 133-4, 166-7
communication maps 57, 152-7
communication matrix 62-3
communication network diagram 63, 64
communication nodes 57
communication officer 105, 158
communication wheel 65
communication Y 66, 72-3, 155
complexity of audit 10
computer data 16
computers 50-1, 92, 159, 163-4
  hardware 96-7, 159
  software 96-7, 159
confidentiality 45
consultant, external
  choice of 9-10
  combined with staff team 11
  interview with CEO 14
consultant auditor 14
content analysis 8, 9, 12, 81-7, 137
  close analysis 83
  80-20 rule of thumb 82
  evaluation 84
  first cut 82-3
  results 84-6, 157-9
  sample categories 83
contract 11, 118
convergence theory 185
corporate culture 5, 6, 86, 97, 113-15, 162, 190
cost of audit 9, 11, 17
cross-group transactions 64
cross-tabulation 50, 53-4, 108, 144-7